Contents

Bryan Turner is Professor of Sociology at the Flinders University of South Australia. He was previously Reader in Sociology at the University of Aberdeen. His publications include *The Dominant Ideology Thesis* (with N. Abercrombie and S. Hill), *Citizenship and Capitalism, Religion and Social Theory,* and *The Body and Society.*

When the bourgeoisie emerged from feudal burgherdom, when this estate of the Middle Ages developed into a modern class, it was always and inevitably accompanied by its shadow, the proletariat. And in the same way bourgeois demands for equality were accompanied by proletarian demands for equality. From the moment when the bourgeois demand for the abolition of class *privileges* was put forward alongside it appeared the proletarian demand for the abolition of the *classes themselves* — at first in religious form, leaning towards primitive Christianity, and later drawing support from the bourgeois equalitarian theories themselves. The proletarians took the bourgeoisie at its word: equality must not be merely apparent, must not apply merely to the sphere of the state, but must also be real, must also be extended to the social economic sphere.

F. Engels, *Anti-Duhring,* Moscow, Foreign Publishing House, 1959, pp. 146-147.

Editor's Foreword

In this major contribution to social stratification theory, Bryan Turner takes as his theme the tension between the political desire for equality and the sociological fact of inequality, within modern societies. It is a platitude to state that inequality is socially ubiquitous, but it is also necessary to recognize that platitudes express the persistence or taken-for-grantedness of social structures. One of the guiding tasks of sociology, I would argue, is to uncover the mechanisms which reproduce structures of social relationship, however obvious and 'natural' they appear to be.

At first sight, it might appear that the question of whether equality is either possible or desirable is of a speculative, philosophical or even solely political nature. To hope to provide a 'scientific' or objective answer might seem to be futile because of the complexity of the issues, or misconceived because the question is purely evaluative. Yet to take this sort of view is to miss an important point.

Within modern *soi-disant* 'democratic' societies the objective of ontological equality ('all men are created equal') is enshrined in the political constitution. The achievement of other equalities — of opportunity, of outcome, of condition — constitutes the domains around which social and political conflict occur. Thus the specification of equality as sets of social and political objectives becomes of concern to social and political theorists, because it is around such specification that ideology is generated, and social action is constructed. Without an understanding of the varying meanings given to the word 'equality' it is impossible to understand any of the fundamental debates about social differentiation — class, gender, race, ethnic, age stratification, etc.

As Bryan Turner shows so clearly in this book, questions about equality and inequality, and their varying definitions, form the very centre of modern sociology — either as a hidden agenda in theoretical conceptualization, or as the context of empirical inquiries into educational opportunity, social mobility or industrial conflict.

If questions about equality and inequality play such a large part in modern sociology — as both metatheoretical themes, and the subjects of specific studies — this is at least in part a result of the contradiction which lies at the heart of all capitalist democratic societies. Whilst the political system is grounded in appeals to the fundamental political equality of its citizens, the economic system can only continue through competition and inequality in access to material resources. Thus, all capitalist democracies are faced with the problem of reconciling social welfare with economic competition. The generation of wealth is essential to the persistence of democratic societies, but cannot be divorced from questions about its distribution. Economic growth and income or wealth equality may be incompatible objectives.

Whilst economic questions are of central importance to the debate about equality they are by no means the only ones. A major virtue of the present work is Professor Turner's demonstration that the analysis of inequality connects to virtually all the significant themes of modern sociology. In discussing the ideological bases of various forms of inequality, for example, it is most instructive to see how both Weber's sociology of religion and Parsons's voluntaristic theory of action each address specific ideological justifications of forms of social inequality. It is perhaps not surprising that Bryan Turner, as a co-author of a recent and important work on the dominant Ideology debate, should pay close attention to this area of his study. But it does also serve to demonstrate the almost unique centrality of equality/inequality as an organizing dichotomy of modern social thought.

By taking as his theme the sociological implications of the idea of equality, Bryan Turner is able to differentiate, in a way which I believe is quite unique, his discussion of the idea from the more conventional approaches of philosophers or political scientists. His achievement lies in his demonstration of the social layering of concepts of equality/inequality, and in particular the contradictory nature of their constituent elements. The presentation of the ways in which the striving for certain forms of equality generate social inequality at another level provides an effective framework in which to locate stratification and ideological debates.

Whilst Bryan Turner does not discuss specific contemporary events in detail, his treatment of the subject provides much to help us understand the complexities of such struggles for equality as that being waged at the time of writing (1986) in South Africa. Whilst sociology as a discipline can never hope to provide more than a small element of an answer to such hideously complex conflicts, this book can only help to clarify what is at issue. Within the contradictory structure of modern capitalist societies, it is only by the expansion of citizenship rights — as Bryan Turner so ably shows — that inequalities may be reduced. This is currently the major issue in South Africa and one which must be resolved if that unhappy country is to have any future as a society. As Professor Turner says, in a passage which can be taken to apply directly to the contemporary situation in South Africa:

> The forms of equality we enjoy in modern democracy are to some extent the consequences of violent or radical action on the part of subordinate groups to achieve a more equitable distribution of wealth and power.

Peter Hamilton

Preface

This study of equality can be seen as part of a wider inquiry into the character of modern industrial societies in terms of social class and ideology. This broader investigation has been conducted with the help and friendship of Nicholas Abercrombie and Stephen Hill. In this particular study I treat the problem of equality as a specific component of citizenship in capitalism and I am grateful to the sociology workshop at Flinders University for support in earlier discussions concerning universalism and citizenship. I am also grateful to Stewart Clegg and John Western for encouragement during my introduction to Australian society. Over a much longer period, my sociological development has depended considerably on the advice and support I have received from Tom Bottomore, Ernest Gellner, John Urry, John Rex, Roland Robertson and Bryan Wilson. Many of the underlying assumptions of this study were, however, originally inculcated by my first teachers in sociology at the University of Leeds. For intellectual and emotional comradeship, I would like to thank Mike Hepworth, Mike Featherstone and Karen Lane. I also want to thank Peter Hamilton for his patience and encouragement during revision of the original manuscript. For typing and secretarial help, I would like to thank Ina Cooper and Sue Manser of Flinders University. Exaggeration, error and plain falsity are my responsibility alone.

1

The Origins of Equality and Inequality

INTRODUCTION

Sociologists typically write about inequality, not equality. Evidence of the extent and persistence of social inequality is so pervasive in contemporary capitalism that inequality appears to be a rather obvious area for research and social policy. By contrast a book on equality probably requires some justification. As a defence of this inquiry into equality, it is the case that egalitarianism is a crucial principle of modern political struggles and social movements for social change. To ignore equality is to neglect an important moral component of organized social movements for the reform of modern conditions. Of course, sociologists are often pessimistic about the possibilities for significant change in capitalism where existing arrangements of private property, family organization and inheritance remain intact. Although scepticism about the possibilities for social change (such as a radical redistribution of income) is a necessary component of the sociological imagination, pessimism is not a requirement of social science. Indeed, fundamental pessimism is clearly incoherent, since a convinced pessimist, like convinced millenarians, should not write books.

A more powerful sociological argument is that theorists who place a special emphasis on the role of capitalism in the creation and maintenance of inequality are often forced to assume implicitly a nostalgic view of history. At least by implication, they suggest that agrarian feudal people did not experience the degrading poverty and inequality which are characteristic of a society dominated by the market. Alternatively, it is suggested that a future socialist society would eradicate the inequalities of capitalism by abolishing private property and personal privilege. Unfortunately, neither viewpoint is convincing. While class inequalities may be dominant in capitalism, feudalism was based on legal estates, rights of immunity and rigid hierarchies of status. It can be said that inequalities based on difference of economic function in capitalism replaced inequalities based on legal divisions in feudalism. In his classic study of equality, R. H. Tawney argued that citizenship and notions concerning equality of opportunity were associated with the historical decline of legal privilege based on status and birth [1]. To recognize that inequality does not have a *special* relationship to capitalism is important, because it liberates us from a false nostalgia about rural communities as an ancient site of human equality. Some eradication of social inequality is always desirable, and sometimes feasible.

Sociology has always had a close, if conflictual and uncertain relationship to socialism. In the nineteenth century, C. H. Saint-Simon simultaneously laid the foundation for French socialism and sociology. While sociologists argue that inequality is all-pervasive, socialist theories argue that genuine equality cannot be achieved until the central institutions of capitalism (the market, private property, family inheritance and class system) have been destroyed or radically transformed or brought under collective ownership and management. To write a book about equality as a principle operating inside capitalist society would as a result be regarded as a contradiction in terms. In a more technical vocabulary, some socialists suggest that capitalism cannot be reformed from inside by the electoral triumph of the working class over the state; it can only be finally abolished by a revolutionary seizure of the state. This argument is parallel to nostalgia about feudalism, since it tends to suggest that inequality has a special relationship to capitalism and it is very pessimistic about the value of improving the lot of the disprivileged in the contemporary context of capitalist societies.

There are two major difficulties with the socialist critique of reformism. First, if capitalism merely replaced the legal inequalities of feudalism by inequalities based on economic divisions, we can argue that state socialism (at least as it exists in the Soviet bloc) has replaced economic divisions in capitalism by political power associated with the Party. These state-socialist governments have rewarded political loyalty with a series of political and economic privileges which create and reinforce social inequalities. Secondly, orthodox socialist analysis has to ignore or negate the real improvements which have been achieved by the working class in Western capitalism as a result of welfare provisions and social security in the post-war period. For example, Sweden under a system of welfare capitalism has enjoyed the lowest infant mortality rates and the highest life expectancy of any society in modern times; Sweden also has an egalitarian system of health care [2]. By suggesting that real improvements in living conditions must await the arrival of genuine socialism, socialist critiques of capitalism in fact become conservative by suggesting that the *status quo* will only be changed by revolutionary action in the future. Why should the working class and other disprivileged sectors of society forego real improvements in welfare, brought about by some modest redistribution of wealth, in anticipation of a distant and uncertain revolution of society?

The final justification for this study is that we live in a period of economic recession when both in principle and in practice the egalitarian aspects of democratic-welfare capitalism are under attack. Having experienced a long period in Britain from the Reform Acts of the Victorian era to the welfare state of the post-war boom, when citizinship rights promoting equality were expanded, social rights are now threatened by the revival of individualism, competition and achievement as dominant values for legitimating welfare cuts, income inequality and high unemployment under a policy of economic monetarism. The struggle for equality as a civilized value is once more at the centre of political conflict. Furthermore, to argue for equality is not sociologically naive, since severe inequalities in a society where expectations of welfare and redistribution are still important in the political process will result in increasing urban violence, personal alienation and social instability. Following Machiavelli, we can suggest that governments should either embrace opposition (by promoting more equality) or crush it (by despotic violence); that is, 'A high level of inequality and a regime structure that is neither democratic nor totalitarian appear to be two potent ingredients of a recipe for political instability' [3]. In societies where parliamentary democracy has nurtured expectations that no citizen should be without some basic claim on social resources, the problem of equality becomes closely bound up with the issue of distributive justice [4]. Sociological evidence suggests that, where there is a widespread and prevalent belief that the existing patterns of distribution are grossly unfair, social and political instability may be expected.

While the problem of social equality obviously leads us into a sociological theory about the conditions for social stability, the exact relationship between equality and stability is complex. L. R. Della-Fave has argued that support for egalitarianism will depend on a 'stratification belief system' which includes: a subjective feeling of grievance; a sense that society not the individual is to blame for inequality; a belief that social equality in a differentiated society is compatible with human nature; and a notion that the achievement of equality is feasible and desirable [5]. Whether a sense of deprivation is combined with an articulate view of fairness will to some extent depend on the presence of countervailing ideologies which, for example, suggest that social inequalities are explained by individual differences (in terms of skill, motivation and effort). In short, the discussion of equality brings us, via an analysis of political stability, to the question of ideology in modern society. These topics (the nature of equality, the conditions of social stability, ideology and social movements to bring about greater equality) provide the central features of this inquiry.

EQUALITY AND CITIZENSHIP

Although the question of equality in sociological theory raises considerable difficulty, I shall attempt to state my argument simply and clearly in this opening introduction. Basically, I conceive equality, as a value and as a principle, as essentially modern and progressive. Of course, the debate about equality has gone on for centuries but the special feature of modern societies is that we no longer take inequality for granted or as a natural circumstance of human beings. Under conditions of modern social citizenship, it is inequality not equality which requires moral justification [6]. The principle of equality from the French and American Revolutions has become one of the central planks of all modern forms of social change and of social movements for the reorganization of societies.

Indeed, it is not simply that equality is a modern value; what is more important is the idea that equality can actually be used as a measure of what it is to be modern and of the whole process of modernization. By tradition I mean a social system based upon hierarchy, particularity, fixed social positions and the allocation of esteem and power according to particular and ascribed characteristics of individuals. The traditional arrangement of society especially in feudalism takes particularistic hierarchy as a natural and fixed element of society and of the natural order of things. Modernization by contrast involves initially an emphasis on achievement and on social mobility according to talent and skill rather than according to age or sexual characteristics. It is for this reason that I am asserting that equality, at least in the shape of political egalitarianism, is a fundamentally modern principle associated with the development of the nation-state.

The existence of social inequality is probably as old as human society itself and correspondingly the debate about the nature and causes of inequality is an ancient topic of social philosophy. In classical Greece, Aristotle in *The Politics* clearly distinguished three social classes and furthermore noted significant differences between slaves and free men, and men and women in terms of their rational and civil capacities. In ancient Hindu society according to the classical texts there were four main castes or *varnas*, namely the priests (Brahmans), the warrior class (Kshatriya), the merchants (Vaishya) and the serfs (Shudras). In the Analects of Confucius we find an account of the social structure of China some two and a half thousand years ago where the function and characteristics of various strata in imperial China were clearly set out. In particular, Confucius was concerned to describe the social behaviour appropriate to gentlemen and knights who were expected to display a moral ideal in their courtly lives, an ideal which exemplified a rational and moral orientation to life. In the *Canterbury Tales* which Chaucer wrote around 1386 we find a descriptive account of certain social roles in the medieval period which reflected a clear division of social strata in terms of honour and social importance. Chaucer's perfect knight embodied a set of ideal standards reflecting a social role which was cultivated in terms of ethical behaviour and courage which clearly distinguished the social status of knights against other occupational groups such as the merchants and the pardoner. These examples could be extended at great length but the point is simply to note that various forms of inequality have existed in all known human societies. Social inequality is ubiquitous and long-enduring, giving rise to the notion that inequality is inevitable in social relations. Whether inequality is natural and inevitable has been the focus of social philosophy for many centuries. The nature of social inequality was clearly central to the philosophies of Aristotle and Plato, and it can be argued that the debate over social inequality formed the basis for the emergence of sociology as a modern discipline [7].

While the philosophical debate about equality is undeniably ancient, the problem of social inequality is essentially a modern question arising with the institutions which constitute modern citizenship. The expansion of social rights of citizenship has been inextricably bound up with social movements to establish equality in modern society. Although modern societies may be prepared to acknowledge certain forms of natural difference, they have been forced politically to take the issue of greater social equality seriously, especially equality of opportunity. Modern politics and modern political institutions are constantly subjected to social pressures to expand opportunities equally, irrespective of ethnicity, sexual identity or age. The political pressure for social equality reflects the presence of universalistic values which undermine and deny particular attributes as the determining features of social membership. Equality is a fundamentally modern value in the sense that universalistic citizenship has become the central feature of political ideology in modern industrial democracies.

In the political theory of classical Greece, the advantages of citizenship or participation in the *polis* were clearly acknowledged but participation was limited to a narrow section of Greek society. The modern notion of citizen presupposes the decline of the dominance of hierarchical social structures and the emergence of more egalitarian horizontal social relations between persons who are defined in universalistic terms.

The principle of citizenship expands with the growth of economic markets and the development of the nation-state where political participation is grounded in social membership irrespective of certain particularistic attributes of individuals. Alongside the modern state there is the growth of formal law which equally provides some guarantee of universalistic legal relations. In this respect it is possible to date the modern analysis of equality from the French Revolution of 1789 which developed under the slogan 'liberty, equality and fraternity'. Of course, the French Revolution was initially a social movement on behalf of property rights against a traditional aristocracy and cannot be interpreted as a classless movement for general equality [8]. While the French Revolution was clearly limited in its political scope, it nevertheless provided the modern basis for civil rights as a requirement for social participation on an egalitarian basis. The modern notion of citizenship presupposes some commitment to equality, an emphasis on universalistic norms and a secular system of values to reinforce political claims and social obligations. Within this framework, social inequality was no longer regarded as inevitable and natural.

The American Revolution which began in 1765 with the Stamp Act and concluded with the Declaration of Independence was another significant aspect of the modern evolution of equality as a political standard based upon universalistic social participation [9]. Although the American Revolution was led by property owners in the interests of property, the Revolution nevertheless established the idea that each man was naturally possessed of liberty and happiness on an equal basis. The American Revolution destroyed the conventions and traditions of a more established regime and laid the basis formal political freedom. It was this contrast between the old feudal regime of France and the democratic structure of American society which provided the starting point for A. de Tocqueville's book *Democracy in America* in 1835. De Tocqueville provided a classical analysis of the conflict between individual liberties and social egalitarianism.

For de Tocqueville the principle of equality which undermines traditional distinctions of social status is the central issue of modern democracies. Although he argued that American society had been transformed in institutions and culture by the widespread application of equality, he also felt that individual liberty was threatened by public opinion which he referred to as 'the tyranny of the majority'. The principle of equality destroyed conventional hierarchies but also obliterated individual differences which de Tocqueville thought were the essence of individuality. The American Revolution had undermined the social inequalities of feudal society where the majority was physically and economically exploited by a ruling class but de Tocqueville argued 'I know no country in which there is so little true independence of mind and freedom of discussion as in America'. [10].

The dangers of democratic equality were felt forcefully by J. S. Mill who read *Democracy in America* in the spring of 1835. The problems of majority political rule as described by de Tocqueville prompted Mill to define what he meant by democracy, that is a social order in which the people have security of good government. However, such a social order could only be achieved by the government of the minority over the majority. Mill felt that the universal franchise would bring about a deadening uniformity of belief and practice which would have the consequence of introducing social stagnation in British society. Mill compared the despotism of custom in Asia with the consequences of mass democracy in a modern industrial society. Democracy would undermine individuality and rule out intelligent and educated political leadership [11].

EQUALITY AND REVOLUTION

We can see that the development of the modern notion of equality was closely associated with revolutionary conflicts and emerging nationalism. The modern notion of equality furthermore gave rise to significant anxieties about the conditions for personal liberty and cultured individuality.

The modern notion of equality cannot be divorced from the evolution of citizenship. However, the concept of citizenship needs further elaboration. Following the work of R. H. Tawney on equality and T. H. Marshall on citizenship, I shall conceptualize egalitarian citizenship in terms of three major dimensions [12]. Civil citizenship refers to equality before the law, personal liberty, the right to own property and freedom of speech. In Britain this civil dimension of political membership developed significantly in the eighteenth century. The defence of civil rights was based upon the development of the law courts as the principal area in which individuals were protected from arbitrary control. The second dimension of citizenship is political equality brought about by access to parliamentary institutions. Political citizenship involves the development of electoral rights and access to popular institutions of political control. It was in the nineteenth century that in Britain the development of the franchise, the ballot and secret voting made political citizenship possible. In the twentieth century there has been a further development of social citizenship which attempts to guarantee a basic level of economic and social welfare. Social citizenship requires the institutional apparatus of the welfare state as the guarantor of rights of economic and social wellbeing. In this respect we can see that the principle of equality is simply another dimension of citizenship, where citizenship rights imply that persons should be treated equally, irrespective of their particular attributes. Furthermore, the protection of equality depends upon a range of institutions (the law courts, parliament and welfare agencies), which are the products of political development.

Modern societies are grounded, at least formally, in a value of egalitarian and universalistic treatment which provides criteria for establishing the direction and quality of modernization. This argument recognizes that, while modern societies are empirically unequal, political life is organized around a struggle for greater equality. There is a conflict between the empirical existence of inequality in the market place and the struggle for democratic equality in the political arena. If equality is a measure of political modernization, then we should be able to establish a variety of historical conditions for the emergence of equality as a value. The historical struggle for equality was closely related to the transformation of traditional societies by either democratic or communist revolutions. The destruction of feudalism can be regarded as a basic condition for the emergence of egalitarian forms of politics. In his classical study, *Social Origins of Dictatorship and Democracy*, Barrington Moore argued that the emergence of democratic political systems involved 'a long and certainly incomplete struggle to do three closely related things: (1) to check arbitrary rulers, (2) to replace arbitrary laws with just and rational ones and (3) to obtain a share for the underlying population in the making of rules'. [13]. The democratic process can be viewed as a struggle to destroy pre-modern forms of political absolutism and despotism, and this struggle inevitably involves attempts to change patriarchal relations within the family, the economic exploitation of young children, the continuity of archaic and particularistic forms of human relations, and the rigidity of conventional hierarchical subordination. Democratic modernization expanded the boundaries of civil society to embrace citizens on a universalistic and egalitarian basis. Violent social class struggles which bring about a liquidation of feudal relations are progressive in laying the basis for egalitarian social relationships. Sociologists have conventionally regarded class formation and class conflict as major dimensions of social change and of the formation of modern consciousness.

To some extent Marx provided the framework for this analysis by drawing a contrast between the fragmented awareness of the self-sufficient peasantry and the revolutionary consciousness of the organized working class within the capitalist enterprise. As a consequence of their opposition to capitalist conditions of work, supervision and control, the working class was welded together as a potent form of opposition to capitalist conditions. The mobilization of the working class as a collectivity with a distinctive consciousness of its class position in opposition to the dominant forms of power and exploitation was a necessary condition for the realization of expanded demands for equality. In addition, the aspirations for an increase of egalitarian rights are typically realized in the context of war-time conflict and social disturbance. Whereas Marxists have focused almost exclusively on class struggle as the harbinger of modern societies, the major advances in the social rights of workers in Western societies have often been consquences of a combination of warfare and class struggle. For example, the expansion of working-class rights and also of women's rights was closely tied to the entry of women into the workforce during the First and Second World Wars, and connected to promises to working-class males of better housing and education in the post-war period. Similarly, advances in housing, education, insurance, social security and medical provision were part of a bargain developed between labour and capital under the auspices of extended state intervention in war-time conditions. War, like class struggle, galvanizes protest and resistance at the same time as it promotes sentiments of patriotic unity, at least in circumstances of popular war against authoritarian and fascist regimes. The combination of patriotism and working-class solidarity is a potent force for the realization of the rights of citizenship. Popular wars, like widespread class conflict, tend to erode traditional patterns within the sexual division of labour, patriarchy within the family, the dominance of religion and the privileges of traditional status grounded in inheritance and social custom [14].

A further dimension in modern patterns of social change has been the importance of migration in disturbing and undermining traditional family, political and social relationships. It is possible to distinguish two migratory situations. First is the migration of male workers out of traditional rural cultures and the radicalization of migrant workers through the experience of geographical and social mobility. The second is the case of a society which is constituted by waves of migration, namely white settler capitalist societies. The contradictory features of individual migration have been widely recognized in sociological studies. The radicalization of migrant populations as a result of migratory experience will depend on the type and causes of migration. When migration is brought about by aspirations to improve standards of living, by changing traditional patterns of life, migrants are often an innovative and radical community. When migrant communities suffer social exclusion as a minority group, there may be strong pressures towards struggles for citizenship rights of egalitarian participation. Although conservative forms of migration which would seek to preserve traditional values and institutions are common, migration is a potentially radical component of social change [15]. Societies which are actually constituted by migration are typically modern societies (Canada, Australia, New Zealand and Hong Kong) because cultural pluralism is often corrosive of established attitude, exclusiveness and particularity in the treatment of individuals. Societies which evolve without a feudal background and are shaped by waves of migration tend to have a popular commitment to egalitarianism; established hierarchies and exclusiveness in interpersonal relations are diminished by the presence of popular culture which promotes interpersonal egalitarianism. The progressive dimension of such societies may well be limited by the presence of indigenous aboriginal societies where the conflict between races gives rise to a racist and reactionary social climate. Settler capitalism often produces a colonial situation where class and racial domination may be intensified, but the intensification may be masked by the adoption of modern means of control [16]. Those societies which achieve industrialization without a transformation of their traditional hierarchies by war, class conflict or migration become industrial societies without an egalitarian culture.

In summary, equality is a modern notion and the value of equality can be taken as a criterion of radical social change. Furthermore, the development of equality is closely related to the development of democratic politics. Democratic societies tend to emerge as a consequence of the collapse of feudalism under the effect of class conflict, warfare and migration. Modern societies are committed to the principle of equality and they no longer regard inequality as automatically justifiable or natural or divinely guaranteed. Of course modern societies continue to be empirically unequal, but this inequality is not regarded as necessarily legitimate or inevitable. Indeed the presence of citizenship as a political norm tends to mean that governments have to justify their continuity by reference to the production of wealth and at least some redistribution of this wealth to marginal or disadvantaged social groups. In the post-war period the majority of democratic societies with an industrial basis sought political authority and continuity on some egalitarian principle of redistribution; modern politics have been primarily about welfare and therefore about the partial redistribution of wealth, either indirectly or directly. Modern societies are as a result somewhat contradictory in that they display continuity of inequality in practice, alongside a political commitment to equality in principle. To express this in more elegant terms, modern capitalism is fractured by the contradictory processes of inequality in the market place and political equality at the level of state politics. There is an inevitable contradiction between economic class and the politics of citizenship.

INEQUALITY AND RESISTANCE

The peculiarity of modern societies, however, is the continuity of inequality in practice, despite the new ideology of equality as the basis of social membership and consequently of citizenship. Inequality is ubiquitous, endemic and resistant to social policies aimed at bringing about a substantial measure of equality in practice. Inequality is in fact inevitable and its presence is felt, not only in capitalist society where there is massive inequality of wealth and income, but also in modern socialist society where there has been a considerable redistribution of economic wealth and regulation of economic markets. Inequality is multidimensional and the elimination of one aspect of inequality often leads to an exaggeration of other aspects of social, political and cultural inequalities. In the language of sociology, all human societies are characterized by some form of social stratification in terms of class, status and power.

This study is primarily concerned with this contradiction between equality as a general value of modern society and inequality as an empirical fact of all human societies. An important feature of this study is the claim that people struggle to achieve equality, to maintain existing levels of equality and to resist the imposition of new inequalities. In short, I reject the view that people accept inequalities as a legitimate feature of modern society; they are not incorporated by a dominant ideology which would attempt to give normative significance to social inequality [17]. This argument is based upon a conception of social individuals as highly resistant to social training and conditioning; this perspective is consequently opposed to any view of human beings as over-socialized [18]. In terms of social psychology, as social agents people actively attempt to understand their environment and their social roles in their social milieu [19]. While individual commitment to a belief system is obviously produced by group affirmation and reward, it is also the case that individuals are highly resistant to change [20]. Furthermore, the socialization of people into a social system is never entirely successful [21].

Human beings resist cultural indoctrination and consciously develop oppositional views of the social structure. They mobilize the notion of equality (implicit and explicit in modern political institutions) in order to assert and realize their own interests. I also argue that the notion of equality as equity is an emergent principle which follows from the basic structure of everyday social exhange and social reciprocity. Within the life-world, there is an imminent value of equal exchange and social reciprocity which develops out of the endless and infinite social exchanges of our daily lives. There is a norm of proportionality in everyday life which flows from the constant round of symbolic and calculative exchanges. While inequality may be endemic to social life, a sense of justice also springs out of the basic reciprocity of social relations. E. Durkheim expressed the view in *The Division of Labour in Society* that the reciprocal nature of exchange is a fundamental basis of social stability in modern society, where there is an extensive social division of labour [22]. This produces an endless conflict between our experience of inequality and our sense of the moral value of equality of exchange. Social inequality is a source of conflict and instability in social relations.

CONTRADICTIONS OF CAPITALISM

The sociology of equality as a value and process in modern society should consequently be seen as another contribution to the conventional problem in sociology of how to explain social order and stability in contemporary societies. Capitalist society is often seen as the naked, competitive conflict between separate individuals who struggle to gain a total control over resources and social wealth. Robinson Crusoe is consequently often held up as the perfect image of the individual in modern industrial society. In a more sophisticated version of this argument, it is often claimed that possessive individualism is the central ideology of industrial capitalist society [23]. If we think of capitalist society by the analogy of a competitive race, then individualism as an ideology is often associated with the principle of equality of opportunity and the idea of a society open to the talents. A society open to the talents is still of course an unequal society, since not everyone can win the race in an open competition. In economic theory this competitive individualism is frequently expressed through an emphasis on the importance of entrepreneurship and the achievement motive for driving the economy. Capitalism and the free market, when combined with institutions of equality of opportunity, produce a society which is radically unequal, despite the existence of an economic surplus.

However, those who are disadvantaged by capitalist relations, or those who are marginal to society as a whole, typically organize together to change the conditions of competition in order to provide themselves with better opportunities and a higher standard of living. Social movements of protest, the trade union movement, workers' associations and associations for disprivileged groups bring pressure to bear on governments in democratic societies in order to change the rules of distribution whereby they might no longer suffer the disadvantages of naked competition. In short, these social groups press for changes in the social structure through the norms of equality of condition and equality of outcome. A good example of this situation is the feminist movement which has sought to bring about a programme of positive discrimination in favour of women in order to get more women into high-status occupations, the educational system and the spheres of influence and control in modern societies. We can see modern society therefore as a struggle between individualism and opportunity on the one hand (in association with monetarist economics) and equality of condition and outcome (in association with Keynesian economics or welfare socialism) on the other. More precisely, capitalism represents an unstable relationship between market forces and stratification as the primary mechanisms of inequality, and political democracy and citizenship as the main expression of equality [24].

Capitalism is a relatively unstable and incoherent social system, because it is based upon the contradictory relationship between equality which is fundamental to its political structure and inequality which is the basis of its economic system. The dilemma of capitalism is intensified because there is a demand for greater equality of condition and outcome, which has often been combined with en expectation of rising standards of living. Modern social movements employing the discourse of citizenship, demand a redistribution of wealth via changes in the system of taxation and inheritance. But there is also the demand for improvement in the standard of living. Wealth has to be more equally distributed but also increased. Although modern capitalism is typically criticized for its inequality and for its exploitation of the natural environment, capitalism has been relatively successful by comparison with state-socialism in generating wealth as an economic surplus to be reinvested to create further economic growth. As Marx constantly noted, capitalism is the most revolutionary economic system yet to appear in history and, through constant technical and organizational changes, generates a vast economic surplus. However, where the market dominated, this wealth was unequally distributed, being accumulated by the owners of property or by those social classes closely associated with economic ownership. Modern capitalism is in terms of wealth, property and income a very unequal social system.

There is a tension, if not a contradiction, between the economic generation of wealth in capitalism and political demands for equality and higher standards of living. The governments of modern capitalist societies are exposed to popular demands for the redistribution of wealth and for institutional changes to create greater educational opportunities because they require electoral support to survive. Governments are also sensitive to demands for improvements in health and general welfare. Governments attempt to raise finance to support welfare institutions through taxation, but taxation represents for the capitalist a threat to profit and a burden on economic production. There are important tensions between the taxation system imposed by governments and the quest for profit on the part of capitalists. A number of social thinkers have seen this contradiction between taxation and profitability as an important aspect of the fiscal crisis of modern governments which cannot be resolved without a certain destabilization of the political system [25].

The problem of reconciling the demands of citizenship with the need for profitability has been intensified in the post-war period by the fact that individual governments can no longer exercise significant control over the economy. This situation has arisen as a consequence of the globalization of the capitalist economy with the increasing importance of multinational corporations. A society like Britain no longer has significant political control over its economic base via its elected government because the British economy is constrained by international economic interests. The problem for the industrial societies of Europe is also that they have suffered a relative economic decline in the 1970s since there has been an important shift of economic power towards the Japanese economy and to some extent to the Pacific Basin generally. While the economic cake is shrinking, these governments are still subject to strong electoral demands for retaining existing standards of living and, where possible, improving these standards. These contradictory pressures at least partly explain the shifting economic policies of British governments between monetarism and Keynesianism.

This sociological study of equality is as a result concerned with the tensions which exist between the demand for equality as expressed through the political process and the facts of inequality that emerged through the market mechanism within capitalist society. However, the demand for equality is empty where there is no wealth to redistribute. The principle of egalitarian citizenship has to be married to an economic system which will produce wealth and furthermore produce expanding wealth in a society where there is a political expectation of rising standards of living. The historical experience of capitalist societies, however, has been that epochs of rapid economic growth in a system of private property ownership have been periods of increasing *relative* inequality, despite a general rise in the standard of living.

THE ORIGINS OF INEQUALITY

In the eighteenth and nineteenth centuries, a number of social philosophers were concerned with the origins, that is the historical roots of human inequality. The most significant contributions to this debate were from writers like J. J. Rousseau, A. Ferguson and J. Millar. While modern sociologists have in general been far less concerned with the issue of the historical origins of human inequality, a significant and valuable contribution to his debate has come from R. Dahrendorf who in his essay 'On the origin of inequality among men' saw himself addressing a problem which had its origins in Rousseau's famous analysis of the character of the social contract and the origins of human inequality [26]. Following Rousseau, Dahrendorf makes a distinction between natural and social differences and further argues that we should distinguish between inequalities that involve some form of evaluative rank order and those types of inequality which do not. It is clear and incontestable that human individuals differ from each other in terms of natural features and natural capability. Some humans are tall, while others are small; some individuals have dark hair and others have blonde hair. We can regard these as natural differences of kind, but there will also be natural differences of rank. This is, some individuals can run faster than others, while some individuals would be able to see further than others. The colour of one's eyes is a matter of natural difference, but the capacity to see great distances is a question of natural rank.

The same distinction between differences of kind and of rank can also apply in social terms. First we should note the existence of social differentiation of social roles which does not necessarily involve any evaluative distinction. Social differentiation is equivalent to the idea of role specification which can be defined in terms of 'those distinctions which take the form of neutral, that is, non-evaluative and non-comparative specifications of the responsibilities and rights attached to a given social position (e.g. father) or of the attributes and qualities assigned to a social type (e.g. woman, man, etc.)'. [27]. In all human societies there will be different tasks and responsibilities assigned to different positions in a society, but this differentiation does not necessarily involve social stratification. Social stratification is social differentiation plus evaluation in terms of reputation, status or wealth. This is, social stratification involves the rank ordering of social positions in terms of some set of hierarchies relating to reputation and wealth. When sociologists consider the nature of inequality, they are primarily concerned with this final form of social distinction, namely the stratification of social positions in terms of rank. Sociologists typically deny that there is any connection other than a contingent one between natural and social inequality. More importantly, they are not particularly interested in the possibility of such a connection. Sociologists are properly concerned with the character of social inequality, irrespective of any alleged correlation or origin in nature. What people mean by the word 'nature' is itself highly problematic, since sociologists would wish to argue that nature is itself a social category and that the term 'nature' is part of a special discourse for the organization of human experiences. For example, is the human body part of nature or part of society? There are strong reasons for believing that the body is the product of endless social practices [28]. Sociologists do, of course, take note of the fact that human societies often attempt to justify and to explain social inequalities by reference to nature in suggesting that all social inequality is derived from the natural inequalities of individuals. I shall be concerned with these issues in Chapter 4 of this study.

The problem of the origins of inequality for sociologists is a question of the social as opposed to natural roots of inequality. We are concerned to understand how inequalities emerge out of the social process and social institutions of any given social system. Dahrendorf's explanation of the social origins of inequality draws upon the tradition of Durkheim and T. Parsons, and puts a special emphasis on the idea of human society as a moral community. At least part of the regulation of human society depends upon the existence of standards or norms. A social role may be defined as a set of expectations relating to a position in a society, a set of expectations which regulates the behaviour of people occupying such positions. A social role may therefore be defined in terms of the norms which determine the proper performance of certain activities. In sociological theory, a social role has three components: it is defined by prescriptions for behaviour, it is socially defined and it is binding on the individual [29]. A school teacher is a social position involving prescriptions regulating the proper behaviour of a teacher. The existence of social norms and social roles necessarily implies the existence of social deviance. That is, the empirical behaviour of a school teacher will from time to time deviate from the norms which define this social position. Wherever there are standards, there will be deviations from them and this is the basic meaning of the common argument that it is the law which produces crime, not crime which produces law. Wherever there is deviance, there will be evaluation since deviance is the product of such evaluations of behaviour and performance.

The importance of this argument for our inquiry into inequality is that it is this evaluation of deviance which produces one necessary form of inequality in all human societies. There will be an inequality of rank resulting from the sanctioning of behaviour according to its conformity with established norms. The existence of social inequality is the product of sanctions, norms and power in social relations. To quote from Dahrendorf's own essay on this issue, we can argue that 'evaluative differentiation, the ordering of social positions and their incumbent scales of prestige or income, is effected only by the sanctioning of social behaviour in terms of normative expectations. Because there are norms and because sanctions are necessary to enforce conformity of human conduct, there has to be inequality of rank among men' [30]. In this sense we can argue that social inequality is inevitable because it is endemic to the very constitution of human society.

Sociologists have been concerned to understand the nature of social inequality since the origins of sociology itself. Indeed, we can virtually define the core of sociology as an inquiry into the origins, characteristics and consequences of social inequality defined in terms of power, status and class. I have argued that sociologists have rarely addressed the question of the origins of our sense of equality. As sociologists we should be concerned to understand this phenomenon precisely because of its contradictory relationship to the empirical inevitability of inequality. I have suggested that we might discover the sense of equality in the very basis of human interaction conceived in terms of exchange. If inequality is endemic to society, we should also note that our sense of equality also grows out of the very fabric of social relations. One important perspective on reciprocity emerged out of the sociology of Durkheim. Towards the conclusion of his study, Durkheim wrote, 'if the division of labour produces solidarity, it is not only because it makes each individual an exchangist, as the economists say; it is because it creates among men an entire system of rights and duties which link them together in a durable way, . . . the division of labour gives rise to rules which assure pacific and regular concourse of divided functions . . . but it is not enough that there be rules; they must be just, and for that it is necessary for the external conditions of competition to be equal' [31].

In attempting to argue that a sense of equality is endemic to social relations I shall follow the tradition of Durkheim and Parsons arguing that our notions of reciprocity are social rather than hedonistic, calculating and individual. Social exchanges in the everyday world involve the sharing of common values of which our sense of justice is a primary feature. All social interaction involves exchange (whether of symbolic entities or commodities) and this infinite process of exchange takes place within a culture which regulates exchange in terms of normative standards. The norm of justice emerges out of everyday life but also structures and guides that everyday world. Our sense of justice grows from the density of ordinary exchange, but our sense of reciprocity is also inculcated from the wider culture of legal norms relating to equality and fairness.

Inequality has its origin in the norms which guide social action. Inequality does not have a special and privileged relationship to capitalism, although class inequalities are fundamental to capitalist societies. A sense of equality emerges out of the reciprocities of everyday life. However, within a broader historical framework, the development of institutions which attempt to produce and maintain social equality was simply part of the rise of modern citizenship. The importance of this argument is that it provides a framework for seeing equality as basic to everyday life, alongside the empirical inequality of rank and status. Although inequality may be inevitable, the notion of fairness, reciprocity and justice is also part of the very fabric of the social reality which we inhabit. The conflict between our sense of fairness and the reality of mundane inequality shapes the elementary forms of our social world. The tension demands both explanation and justification.

REFERENCES

[1] R. H. Tawney, *Equality*, London, Allen & Unwin, 1931. For additional commentary, R. H. Tawney, *The Attack and Other Papers*,

London, Allen & Unwin, 1953; R. H. Tawney, *The Radical Tradition*, London, Allen & Unwin, 1964.

[2] E. Mumford, *Medical Sociology, patients, providers and politics*, New York, Random House, 1983, pp. 478–479.

[3] E. N. Muller, 'Income inequality, regime repressiveness and political violence', *American Sociological Review*, **50**(1), 1985, p. 60.

[4] L. Rainwater, *What Money Buys*, New York, Basic Books, 1974.

[5] L. R. Della-Fave, 'On the structure of egalitarianism', *Social Problems*, **22**, 1974, pp. 199–213.

[6] I. Berlin, 'Equality', *Proceedings of the Aristotelian Society*, New Series, **56**, 1956, pp. 301–326.

[7] R. Dahrendorf, 'On the origin of inequality among men' in *Essays in the Theory of Society*, London, Routledge & Kegan Paul, 1968, pp. 151–178.

[8] T. Skocpol, *States and Social Revolutions, a comparative analysis of France, Russia, China*, Cambridge, Cambridge University Press, 1979.

[9] C. Brinton, *The Anatomy of Revolutions*, New York, Vintage Books, 1965.

[10] A. de Tocqueville, *Democracy in America*, London, Oxford University Press, 1946, p. 192.

[11] B. S. Turner, 'The concept of social "stationariness": utilitarianism and Marxism', *Science and Society*, **38**(1), 1974, pp. 3–18.

[12] T. H. Marshall, *Class, Citizenship and Social Development*, Chicago & London, Chicago University Press, 1977; T. H. Marshall, *The Right to Welfare and Other Essays*, London, Heinemann, 1981.

[13] Barrington Moore, *Social Origins of Dictatorship and Democracy. lord and peasant in the making of the modern world*, Harmondsworth, Peregrine Books, 1969, p. 414.

[14] R. T. Titmuss, *Essays on 'The Welfare State'*, London, Unwin University Books, 1958.

[15] J. A. Jackson (ed.), *Migration*, Cambridge, Cambridge University Press, 1969, and W. Petersen, 'A general typology of migration', *American Sociological Review*, **23**, 1958, pp. 256–265.

[16] S. Greenberg, *Race and State in Capitalist Development, Comparative Perspectives*, New Haven, Yale University Press, 1980.

[17] N. Abercrombie, S. Hill and B. S. Turner, *The Dominant Ideology Thesis*, London, Allen & Unwin, 1980.

[18] D. H. Wrong, 'The oversocialized conception of man in modern sociology', *American Sociological Review*, **26**, 1961, pp. 183–193; A. Dawe, 'The two sociologies', *British Journal of Sociology*, **21**(2), 1970, pp. 207–218; A. Giddens, *The Constitution of Society*, Oxford,

Polity Press, 1984, Ch. 1; N. Abercrombie, S. Hill and B. S. Turner, 'Determinacy and indeterminacy in the theory of ideology', *New Left Review*, No. 142, 1983, pp. 55–66.

[19] F. Heider, *The Psychology of Interpersonal Relations*, New York, Wiley, 1958.

[20] J. T. Borhek and R. F. Curtis, *A Sociology of Belief*, New York, John Wiley, 1975.

[21] N. Abercrombie, *Class, Structure and Knowledge*, Oxford, Blackwell, 1980, pp. 159ff.

[22] E. Durkheim, *The Division of Labour in Society*, London, Collier–Macmillan, 1964, Ch. 3.

[23] C. B. Macpherson, *The Political Theory of Possessive Individualism, Hobbes to Locke*, Oxford, Clarendon Press, 1962; D. F. B. Tucker, *Marxism and Individualism*, Oxford, Blackwell, 1980.

[24] T. H. Marshall, *The Right to Welfare and Other Essays*, London, Heinemann, 1981.

[25] J. O'Connor, *The Fiscal Crisis of the State*, London, St. James Press, 1973; J. Habermas, *Legitimation Crisis*, London, Heinemann, 1974.

[26] R. Dahrendorf, op. cit. For further comment R. Dahrendorf, *Essays in the Theory of Society*, London, Routledge & Kegan Paul, 1968.

[27] M. M. Tumin, 'On Inequality', *American Sociological Review*, **28**(1), 1963, p. 14.

[28] B. S. Turner, *The Body and Society, explorations in Social Theory*, Oxford, Blackwell, 1984, Ch. 10.

[29] R. Dahrendorf, *Homo Sociologicus*, London, Routledge & Kegan Paul, 1973.

[30] R. Dahrendorf, op. cit., p. 172.

[31] E. Durkheim, op. cit., pp. 406–407.

2

Types of Equality

DEFINING EQUALITY

The debate about the relationship between capitalism and inequality, or between politics and economics will hinge crucially on the meaning we give to the notion of equality. Before developing this argument further we need to turn to the complex question of defining equality. Every modern political constitution has some notion of human equality inscribed in its fundamental laws and every modern political theory of any importance has contributed to the debate about the nature and feasibility of social egalitarianism. However, it turned out that equality is almost as difficult to define clearly as it is to achieve politically. There is, however, some consensus concerning the dimensions along with equality should be measured.

It is common to identify four types of equality. The first is ontological equality or the fundamental equality of persons. Secondly, there is equality of opportunity to achieve desirable ends. Thirdly there is equality of condition where there is an attempt to make the conditions of life equal for relevant social groups. Fourthly there is equality of outcome or equality of result [1].

The notion of an ontological equality between human beings is common to certain religious and moral traditions. It typically takes the form of an assertion of equality of persons before God; for example, in Christianity there is the notion that all people are equal under the fatherhood of God. In medieval society this tradition was sometimes associated with a natural law position which asserted an essential equality of human beings *qua* human beings. These religious views of an ontological equality of persons have become less important in the modern world as a consequence of secularization and the resulting decline of natural law as a moral framework for the debate about human nature [2]. There is however a modern form of the notion of an equality of human essence which is to be found in the philosophical anthropology of Marxism; in this Marxist tradition it is claimed that all human beings are defined by *praxis*, that is, all human beings are knowledgeable, conscious and practical agents. All human beings have to labour productively to produce their means of existence and to reproduce their own species. From this point of view it is asserted that 'man is by his essence a universal free being who forms himself through his own self activity in the direction of an ever widening mastery of nature and an ever more universal intercourse, autonomy and consciousness' [3]. Writers like R. H. Tawney often combined socialism and Christianity to provide a religious foundation for a commitment to social equality [4]. Both conventional Christianity and humanist Marxism have been challenged by the highly relativistic forms of modern social thought which would see human nature as specific to certain cultures and social systems. Within this relativistic perspective it is difficult to isolate any specific form of human attribute which could be shared universally amongst the whole human race. Indeed it is problematic to identify any attribute at all which is held in common by the human species. The argument for an ontological equality is somewhat rare in modern egalitarianism.

Within the Western democratic tradition the most common argument for equality is typically couched in terms of an equality of opportunity and equality of condition. The notion of equal opportunity is relatively easy to understand. In principle it means that access to important social institutions should be open to all on universalistic grounds, especially by achievement and talent. The idea of a career open to talent was an important legacy of the French and American Revolutions which asserted that major administrative and professional positions in society should be filled by persons of talent regardless of their birth or social background. The debate about equality of opportunity was especially important in the development of modern educational institutions where promotion and attainment are in theory based upon intelligence, skill and talent regardless of parental and class background. This feature of educational theory gave rise to an important notion in modern social theory, namely that of meritocracy. In a meritocracy positions in the occupational structure of a society would be filled on the basis of personal merit, in terms of universal criteria of achievement, not on ascribed standards of age, sex or wealth [5].

The concept of equality of opportunity is closely related to and somewhat inseparable from the notion of equality of condition. Equality of opportunity rewards those who have ability and who are prepared to exercise their skills in the interest of personal achievement in a competitive situation. However, where parents can pass on advantages to their children, then the starting-point for achievement is unequal since for example, working-class children will start with disadvantages which they have inherited from their parents. In English society, where accent and social standing are significant in terms of social achievement and social acceptance, there are important inequalities which are inherited. Indeed some sociologists using the notion of cultural capital have argued that success in education is primarily dictated by the extent to which individuals have absorbed the dominant culture or how much cultural capital they have acquired [6]. In order for equality of opportunity to have any significant content it is essential to guarantee equality of condition, that is, all competitors in the race should start at the same point with appropriate handicaps.

Finally the most radical notion of equality is equality of result or outcome. The aim here is through legislation and other political means to achieve equalities of result regardless of starting point and natural ability. A program of equality of result would seek to transform inequalities at the beginning into social equalities as a conclusion. Social programs of positive discrimination in favour of disadvantaged or disprivileged groups (such as women, children or ethnic minorities) are meant to compensate for significant inequalities of condition in order to bring about a meaningful equality of opportunity to secure an equality of result.

In summary, ontological equality is an argument closely associated with moral or religious systems, especially traditional Christianity or in more recent times humanistic Marxism. To believe in an equality of human essence requires a strong moral argument which would override our sense of cultural relativity. The notion of an absolute essence of human equality or even a notion of an equality of human potentiality is not common in contemporary arguments in favour of social equality. In liberal and democratic traditions the idea of equality of opportunity and of condition has been fundamental to the development of citizenship where the cultivation of talent and skill through a universal educational system has been an important feature of modern programs of welfare. These forms of equality have been associated with political programs designed to redistribute wealth through tax reform, welfare and other forms of social amelioration. Finally, an equality of outcome has been part of the platform of most socialist policies aimed at redressing the inequalities characteristic of competition and the market place.

ARGUMENTS AGAINST EQUALITY

Having outlined the conventional meaning of equality, we are now in a position to consider some of the common arguments against equality. The case against social equality has been conducted within a restricted framework and the arguments can consequently be expressed relatively simply. The first argument is that the different components of equality are often mutually incompatible. For example, equality of opportunity and condition tend to produce inequality of results. If we imagine society to be a competitive race, then competition inevitably results in inequality of outcome, since not every person in the race can be a winner. The notion of equality of opportunity is characteristic of liberalism and some versions of liberalism are content to accept a social situation where inequality of outcome is predominant. One argument against equality therefore concentrates on the philosophical incoherence or at least incompatibility between the various features of the modern doctrine of social equality [7].

The second and more interesting argument against equality is that a political program to secure social equality generally would be infeasible, since to secure radical equality of condition or equality of outcome would require massive social and political regulation by the state resulting in a totalitarian and authoritarian regime. The price of significant equality is political despotism which would subordinate individual talent and achievement. Radical equality of persons and outcome requires a totalitarian system of regulation but, some political and social theorists would argue that totalitarianism is itself infeasible. In practice so-called totalitarian regimes have never achieved total regulation of human populations, since human beings are resistant to such absolute regimentation and no system of authoritarian politics has ever managed to subordinate individuals in an entirely totalitarian fashion [8]. Less dramatically, it would be difficult for a society to provide continuously the level of bureaucratic regulation and social investigation which a program for equality of results would necessitate, at least without massive economic and political conflict. Some degree of inequality of outcome appears to be inevitable despite all social and political attempts to eradicate such inequalities. Regardless of its philosophical content, the idea of absolute equality is sociologically problematic.

The third argument against equality is that some forms of radical equality are not desirable, since the achievement of equality may be incompatible with other values which are also desirable. For example, it is very commonly argued that equality is less desirable then personal liberty, or at least that liberty and equality are somewhat mutually exclusive. For example, the regulation of the economy and social life which would be required to bring about equality of condition or equality of outcome would limit certain personal freedoms and conflict with a strong doctrine of liberty.

Some aspects of the argument against equality are problematic from a sociological perspective. For example, the liberal argument that equality and freedom are mutually incompatible has to assume an inevitable and necessary conflict between personal interest and social requirements. Liberalism poses a false dichotomy between the individual and society. Such a philosophical position is sociologically questionable, since the achievement of personal satisfaction is typically possible only in the context of a supportive social environment. For example, the educational development of the individual to a level of sophisticated consciousness requires a long educational history which may only be possible where society provides open access to educational institutions. To become a self-conscious, reflective and educated individual is essentially a social process, so that the liberal opposition between the person and the society is questionable. It is for this reason that we can appreciate the fundamental relationship between social citizenship, equality and individual development. The enhancement of individual potential in modern societies has been made possible by the extension of citizenship rights on a universalistic basis and the liberty of the individual to develop educationally requires state intervention to redistribute wealth in a way which makes possible general education. There is no inevitable conflict between liberty and equality since, as R. Dahrendorf made clear, 'citizenship rights alone make the chance of liberty available to those who are least favourably placed in the hierarchy of social differentiation' [9]. The traditional philosophical discussion of the possibilities of personal freedom and social equality fails to take account of the sociological dimension to this contrast in the specific circumstances of late capitalist society. The conflict between personal freedom and social regulation reflects a structural difference between the competitive economic struggle of the market place and the political process of democracy at the level of the state. There is a contradiction between personal achievement in terms of market possibilities and the social requirement of economic and political regulation which is aimed at minimizing the anarchic effects of naked economic struggle.

There is a conflict between the economic inequalities which flow from the economy and the democratic requirements for social equality which are necessitated by the political process of voting and government election. Governments are forced to appeal to the electorate in terms of welfare and social improvement while ensuring that the economy continues to function in a competitive and expanding fashion. The problem of modern government is to satisfy the needs of citizens in an open democratic process while continuing to support the economy. Profitability of investment in a system of private property conflicts with the requirements of redistribution in a policy guided by democratic values.

In examining the traditional arguments against equality, I have been primarily concerned with certain philosophical traditions which would see equality as incoherent, not feasible and not desirable. The philosophical critique of equality is often mainly concerned with certain conceptual and terminological problems in the egalitarian ideal. By suggesting that the problem of equality is in fact a sociological problem, I have begun to open up a new dimension to the issue of social equality, namely the relationship between political and economic processes. Although social philosophy has often questioned the possibility of full equality, there is also an important sociological tradition which has asserted the social significance of inequality or more directly argued that social stratification has an important functional contribution to make to the continuity of social systems. This sociological argument, which is known as the functional theory of stratification, was closely associated with the sociological perspective of T. Parsons, K. Davis and W. E. Moore [10].

FUNCTIONAL THEORY OF STRATIFICATION

The basic components of the functionalist theory of social stratification can be stated simply in the following terms. In any society, some social positions are functionally more important than others in the sense that they significantly contribute to the maintenance and continuity of the whole social system, and therefore require special skills for their performance. In any society only a limited number of individuals have the skills and talent which are required to perform these social functions; these talents can be trained into the skills appropriate to these functional positions only over a significant period. The transformation of talents into social skills requires a training period of some duration involving sacrifices made by those undergoing the training. To encourage talented persons to undergo sacrifices during a period of training, these functional positions must carry a significant inducement in the shape of a social differential, involving privileges and disproportionate access to scarce rewards. There is a hierarchy of rights and prerequisites attached to the functional hierarchy of occupational positions, and these rights involve significant rewards to those undergoing training. This differential access to the fundamental rewards of a society corresponds to the differentiation of prestige and honour which various social strata acquire. In short, societies are stratified in terms of rights and rewards which induce people to undergo sacrifices and training for social roles which are demanding while also being rewarding. It follows that social inequality among different social strata is positively functional for the continuity and maintenance of society, but also inevitable in all societies where there is a differentiation of social roles [11].

Although social positions are not always rewarded in direct proportion to their functional importance these positions should be sufficiently rewarded to attract competent social agents. The functional theory of stratification thus had two features; firstly it was a theory of occupational rank in terms of functional contributions to the maintenance and continuity of social systems and secondly it was a theory of social motivation whereby functionally demanding social roles would be sufficiently rewarding to attract persons to make the necessary sacrifices in terms of education and commitment.

Finally we should note that the theory carried with it the implication that functional stratification was a universal feature of all social systems and consequently that social inequality was not only ineradicable but actually necessary for the continuity of social life. The functionalist theory of stratification gave rise to an extensive debate [12].

The functional theory of stratification is essentially an argument about the equality of opportunity, because it assumes a fixed ranking of social roles where individuals have to be induced to occupy these positions in return for a number of rewards and privileges. The theory of stratification does not therefore answer the problems raised by either the notion of equality of condition or equality of outcomes. It assumes that the competitive race for social positions has an egalitarian starting point and this assumption is dubious without equality of condition. To be precise, the theory did not allow for such distorting circumstances as the inheritance of cultural capital. The competitive race for social positions is not equal unless there is equality of condition. Secondly, the theory of functional stratification is circular, since those positions which are highly rewarded are functionally important, but the way in which we know which positions are functionally important is by reference to whether they are highly rewarded. To take an example from medical history, there is a good argument that sanitary engineers made a more important functional contribution to the social system than doctors, but doctors are clearly more highly rewarded in terms of finance and prestige than engineers. The rewards which accrue to social positions may well be the outcome of power conflicts and social closure rather than functional importance. Thirdly, the prestige of occupational positions is often maintained by credentialism and social closure to preserve traditional advantages by restricting access to functionally important positions to a limited range of candidates. It could be argued therefore that social stratification is dysfunctional to the maintenance of a social system. Fourthly, it is not self-evident that training for a prestigous occupation is a significant sacrifice since earnings which are forgone may often be recovered relatively quickly once employment has been achieved. In addition, it is typically the case that either parents and/or the state contribute to the training of students for these occupations in a university environment which is relatively pleasant. Fifthly, the argument fails to evaluate alternative systems of occupational placement, motivation and reward within an egalitarian society. Social positions may be rewarding over and above their income by reference to social prestige and intrinsic reward. A number of social roles such as nursing may be regarded as socially important despite their low income and persons who occupy such roles are typically motivated by moral or religious arguments where a direct monetary reward is absent. Finally, the theory suffers from a range of problems which are common to functionalism as such and in particular is faulted by an unsophisticated notion of value consensus. In industrial societies, there has been major conflict over the evaluation of occupational prestige and rewards, but stratification theory does not explain dissensus over the prestige ranking of occupations and their system of rewards. These conflicts over the prestige rating of occupations precisely reflect a basic division over the nature of equality and equity in societies; that is, the disputes are characterized by conflicts over questions of fairness with respect to rewards for difficult or dangerous tasks. The remuneration of employment is normally determined by conflicts in the market place between employers and trade unions and levels of reward are the outcome of quite consistent and open industrial disputes [13].

There are a number of other arguments we should consider which suggest that inequality in economic terms has a number of important social functions both for society and for specific social groups. For example, it can be argued that low pay and associated poverty guarantees that 'dirty work' will be accomplished in an affluent society. If all persons received the same economic wage regardless of their tasks, then dirty or demeaning work would never be accomplished. In association with this argument critics of welfare typically suggest that welfare payments should be well below market rates in order to guarantee that certain forms of economic activity will be sought after by those on low pay. That is, if welfare payments rise above the level of low incomes, there is no real incentive to seek full employment [14]. The stigmatisation of the poor has an important economic function in forcing people to work and contribute to general productivity.

Another argument is that inequalities of wealth are important in subsidizing the living standards of upper and middle classes by making their lives more comfortable and enjoyable. It is also the case that the lower-paid subsidize the public sector because they typically contribute a higher percentage of their income in taxes than more wealthy sectors of the population who can normally avoid taxation by employing the services of accountants and by claiming tax allowances for aspects of their employment. There is also the common situation that the unemployed, the needy and the lower-paid sector of the population do not normally claim their full entitlement to welfare payments precisely because of the stigmatization associated with dependency on the state [15].

There are also a number of somewhat cynical arguments that suggest the functional importance of the poor is also to be found in their contribution to professional employment such as doctors, welfare services, social workers and ministers of religion. Since the poor are the main clients for these groups, the poor function to provide employment for professional groups but also for owners of pawn shops and brothels. There are also economic arguments to the effect that the poor prolong the usefulness of certain items such as day-old bread and fruit, second-hand clothing and poor quality motor cars and dwelling places. Against these arguments in favour of income and economic inequality, H. J. Gans in *More Equality* has provided a range of alternatives whereby the functions of poverty could be replaced by more morally acceptable circumstances or behaviour. For example, dirty work could be done successfully by automation and the use of computerized services; he also believes that higher wages could be offered for essential but dirty work without serious damage to the economy [16].

In general sociologists have argued that some form of inequality (whether of wealth, power or prestige) is inevitable. Sociologists do not generally use the notion of desirability to discuss or describe social inequality, but they have employed the language of functionalism to discuss the effects and consequences of inequality for the continuity or mainten- ance of social systems. There has been massive disagreement as to what would constitute a contribution to social systems by inequality and they have disagreed about how this contribution might be measured. While inequality may be inevitable, the real question centres ultimately on the degree and extent of inequality. That is, it is difficult to conceptualize a social system where inequality was wholly absent or a social system where inequality was manifest at every level of social and personal relations. The debate is focused around the question of the distribution and concentration of resources rather than on the absence or presence of inequality as such. While all social systems may be characterized by various forms of social stratification and inequality, there is considerable variation in the degree of concentration of inequality and as a result debates about equality tend to shift towards questions of equity within the distributive processes of social systems [17]. The argument against inequality has also to take the form of a discussion concerning the scope of concentration of power, privilege and wealth. Within a sociological framework, it is reasonable to conduct an enquiry into the possibility of more equality and less concentration of wealth rather than to pose utopian questions about the total absense of all forms of inequality. Another dimension to this question is the argument that some forms of inequality may be acceptable provided there is sufficient scope for social mobility within a social system. That is, people may be prepared to accept forms of inequality provided there are good opportuni- ties for social promotion, advancement and mobility with respect to talent and skill. The question of equality as a result is finally transformed into a question about fairness, equity and justice.

We may define justice as simply the notion of giving each person his/her due or simply as treating people who are equals equally. Justice as a procedure may be interpreted as treating people impartially according to certain public rules which apply to all. Procedural justice would require the public stipulation of rules and procedures in order to determine whether these were properly followed. In a more interesting fashion, justice may be defined substantively as involving some distributive principle prescribing the dispersion of rights and benefits over a society in order to maximize the advantages of all. Furthermore a distributive principle can also be a *re*distributive principle which would argue that the existing injustices should be equalized by a redistribution of wealth or existing equalities should be maximized by some form of redistribution. The redistributive principle typically involves some taxation, insurance and savings policies designed to counteract the forces of the market place in the interests of justice. The institutional requirements of justice as fairness are relatively obvious, namely a just system of legal institutions, open access to litigation, the availability of public bodies to watch over legal principles and a political system to guarantee obedience to public rules [18]. The redistributive principles of justice are complex, involving problematic relations between the state and the economy.

EQUALITY AND JUSTICE

In his collection of essays published as *A Theory of Justice*, J. Rawls attempted to outline a social theory of justice which would reconcile the liberal tradition of citizenship with a social conception of economic wealth. Rawls argued that a just society would involve the maximization of equal basic liberties where the liberty of one person would not conflict with the liberty of others, and he outlined a set of proposals which would establish a sense of justness and fairness with respect to social and economic inequalities. These inequalities are to be arranged so that they contribute the greatest benefit to the least advantaged and the offices and positions within a society should be open to all under conditions of equality of opportunity [19]. Rawl's general conception of social justice was that all essential social goods should be distributed equally amongst all unless an unequal distribution of these goods would be to the advantage of the least-favoured members of society. The principle is that inequality above the income median is socially desirable from the point of view of justice only when it helps to reduce the inequalities which exist below the median.

Rawl's theory of justice has been influential and significant in the development of both political and economic thinking about social inequality and the interest of the theory lies partly in its attempt to reconcile utilitarian rationalism with the maximum level of personal liberty plus a social principle of redistribution. Within this framework equality is desirable because there is a moral argument in favour of fairness and because this particular principle of justice brings about an increasing benefit to all members of society but especially those who are least favoured. Through Rawl's principle of fairness, we can posit the additional argument that equality within a political democracy is essential for the development of an educated and rational electorate which has the opportunity and ability to participate in and discuss public policy making in order to make such processes accountable, effective and efficient. The equalization of citizenship should in this sense enhance individual self-realization since political participation contributes to the growth of political awareness and confidence. More importantly, it has been argued that social equality is a basic condition for political and social stability. In this respect social and economic equality are probably more significant than the political equalities of citizenship. The reduction of inequalities reduces the level of social conflict and tension, encouraging greater cooperation between social groups and developing a widespread sense of the legitimacy of society. Citizenship functions to reduce the level of political tension and violence within the social system [20]. In terms of T. H. Marshall's view of citizenship, the growth of social welfare via the intervention of the state in response to trade union and political activity brings about an abatement of class conflicts following from the inequalities of reward and ownership in the market place.

The theory that the reduction of economic and social deprivation brings about a greater sense of justice in society which has the consequence of minimizing social conflict and political violence can be challenged on the grounds that most industrial democratic societies are very unequal but this has not brought about significant political or social violence. In Great Britain in 1949 the top 10 per cent of the population enjoyed 33 per cent of the total distribution of income before taxation, but in 1977 the top 10 per cent enjoyed 28 per cent of income before taxation. This apparent redistribution had not, however, brought about a significant improvement of the bottom 30 per cent of the population, since this redistribution had been primarily enjoyed by the middle class. In America a similar situation obtains, where in 1947 the top 20 per cent enjoyed 46 per cent of income before taxation and in 1972 this had been reduced to 44 per cent; the share going to the bottom 20 per cent had not changed at all during this period [21]. Inequalities in other resources (such as education and health) have also been retained despite the development of welfare policies. These continuing inequalities have led certain writers to conclude that reformism has basic limits since all industrial democratic societies have been characterized by continuing inequality despite reformist legislation [22].

In terms of Rawl's theory of justice, the continuity of income inequality could still be regarded as fair on the condition that offices and positions within the society were open to all in terms of some impartial test of talent and ability. In short, social inequality may be regarded as fair provided there is rapid or open social mobility. The majority of commentators on social mobility have all argued that justice, democracy and citizenship are impossible without social mobility and that the stability of modern industrial societies depends crucially on the availability of mass education as the avenue for social advancement. In Britain the debate about social mobility has been complex, divided and acrimonious. One famous study of social mobility was conducted by D. Glass in 1949 [23]. Glass came to three conclusions, which were that most mobility in Britain is short range, there is a barrier to social mobility across the manual and non-manual division and finally there is a high level of self-recruitment in the upper classes. The Glass survey was welcomed by Marxist sociologists who interpreted these data as indicating that the myth of classlessness was finally destroyed in social science, seeing these forms of inequality as confirmation of Marx's analysis of class in capitalism [24]. It is obviously the case that the Glass findings are incompatible with a view of Britain as a society in which social citizenship has become a significant feature of social life, expanding the boundaries of social participation and providing the conditions for an egalitarian society.

More recent research on social mobility in Britain has, however, seriously questioned Glass's earlier findings and laid the basis for an entirely different view of equality in Britain. In the so-called Oxford Mobility Enquiry, J. Goldthorpe and his colleagues, on the basis of a substantial sample of adult males in 1972 in England and Wales, came to some conclusions which were largely the opposite of those originally established by the Glass enquiry [25]. Goldthorpe's survey results showed that Britain was a society with relatively high social mobility and that individual positions in the class structures were not fixed at birth. In Britain there is considerable long-range mobility from the lower to the upper classes as well as considerable short-range mobility. Membership of the higher 'service' and intermediate classes is more fluid than expected. There is more upward than downward mobility because there is more room at 'the top' as a consequence of the development of professional, service and quasi-professional classes, especially those associated with government employment [26]. Although Goldthorpe's research can be criticized on a variety of grounds, the survey material on mobility in Britain in the post-war period would suggest that, while Britain remains an unequal society, there is considerable social mobility which is partly associated with a growth in white-collar employment and an expansion of the middle class [27].

EDUCATIONAL EQUALITY

Equality of opportunity depends upon, among other things, open access to educational institutions on an equal basis to facilitate social mobility. Although some authors argue that educational attainment reflects intellectual ability (as measured for example by IQ tests), sociological research demonstrates that, when IQ is held constant, there are important variations between social groups in terms of educational attainment. For example, in *The Home and the School*, J. W. B. Douglas found that 'high ability' students from different social classes had significantly different results in their examinations, with ability held constant. Douglas found that working-class children left school much earlier than middle class children [28], and referred to this loss of talent from the secondary and tertiary system as a 'wastage of ability'. He explained this wastage of talent in working-class children as a consequence of a cumulative process of deprivation from poor housing, inadequate cultural environment, attendance at schools with a low level of success, admission to lower streams in schools and lack of support from parents. The crucial factor in this ensemble of deprivation was the level of parental interest in the school performance of the child.

The findings of Douglas's research have been confirmed and elaborated subsequently in the sociology of education in Britain. One tradition of inquiry into classroom interactions suggested that the deprivation of the children within the wider community was reproduced in the classroom setting [29]. These studies argued that, in addition to a formal curriculum, schools have a hidden curriculum which induces the children to accept social controls, their place in society and the assumption that inequalities are natural and inevitable. The streaming of schools creates distinctive school subcultures which teach children to accept the stereotypical classification of children into 'able' and 'less able' groups. Within this system, the educational attainment of pupils is the outcome not simply of intelligence but also of social arrangements within the classroom and the school.

The general conclusion of educational sociology in Britain and elsewhere is that the school and the family tend to reproduce the social inequalities of the class system within the wider society. B. Bernstein for example has argued that class differences in speech codes also partly account for variations in school performance and educational attainment.

Middle-class children acquire from their own homes an elborated speech code which is highly congruent with the language patterns which prevail in the school [30]. By contrast, working-class children have a restricted speech code which is characterized by simplicity and directness rather than by scope and generality. This restricted code is a distinct disadvantage in the school setting.

The theory of cultural deprivation is important for explaining differences in educational achievement when ability is held constant, but it has been criticized because, at least by implication, it lays the final blame for failure on the child and the family. The educational system and the social elite which it serves remains beyond criticism [31]. In reply to cultural deprivation and classroom interaction theories, R. Boudon suggests that, even if children were not exposed to subcultures in the school, they would still be disadvantaged as a consequence of their location in the general system of stratification [32]. Boudon concludes that inequality in educational opportunity could only be eliminated if the society became unstratified or the school system was totally undifferentiated. Neither outcome appears likely in Western societies and therefore inequalities in education and occupational mobility will persist. Social inequality is maintained by a functional circle which connects class differences to the school system, to the persistence of classroom subcultures and to the cultural expectations which operate in the home [33].

In his review of recent trends in British society, A. H. Halsey came to a similarly pessimistic view about the post-war achievement of equality of opportunity. Although there has been an expansion of educational provision and an improvement of standards,

> the anticipated greater equality of access to the national heritage has not materialized. Thresholds have certainly been raised and the area of free secondary education has been expanded under the auspices of the state. But the further activity of the state in expanding educational opportunity beyond the statutory leaving age has provided additional opportunities which have, at least into the 1960s, been seized disproportionately by those born into advantageous class circumstances. [34]

The result is that the occupational hierarchy provides rewards for successful university students, thereby reinforcing the relationship between advantage at birth and social mobility through university certification. In Britain, nine out of every ten male university graduates successfully entered the managerial and professional classes. These conclusions clearly support the argument at the beginning of this chapter that an expansion of educational opportunity would not necessarily expand social equality because equality of opportunity is relatively insignificant without equality of conditions. In addition, equality of opportunity may stand in a contradictory relationship to equality of outcome.

In addition, in the British context, educational conservatives have questioned the basic assumptions of state provision, especially the value of a comprehensive education at the secondary level. Those social groups which want to attack the dominance of the state in educational provision have mobilized the liberal perspective on free choice, parental authority and pluralism to achieve state support to finance an expansion of the private sector. These developments have been especially crucial in the growth of denominational schools. The trend towards a privatization of schooling will tend to reinforce the prevailing inequalities in the school system and within the wider society. In the industrial capitalist societies, the government and other elites are recruited overwhelmingly from the private school sector. In Britain, sociological evidence from the 1950s and 1960s showed that between 70 and 87 per cent of Conservative cabinet members, judges, ambassadors and governors of the Bank of England had been recruited from the independent public schools, especially Eton, Harrow and Winchester [35]. Although recruitment to the Civil Service by open examination has shown a decline in the representation of independent school entrants (from 80 per cent in 1909–1914 to 51 per cent in 1956–63), this is less impressive when we consider the substantial expansion of grammar school education after the 1944 Education Act [36]. To consider a comparative picture from Australia, 43 per cent of Australian-educated elites had been recruited from 23 schools operating in the period 1930s and 1940s. Of these schools, 18 belonged in 1975 to the Headmaster's Conference of the Independent Schools in Australia. These 18 schools provided one-third of the educational elite of Australia [37]. Research on elite recruitment merely confirms the general argument that the development of formal criteria of recruitment on the basis of universal standards of performance will not radically transform patterns of inequality in the absence of additional changes within the prevailing system of power and stratification [38].

POLITICAL RADICALISM AND EQUALITY

Whether or not people feel a significant level of dissatisfaction and alienation from a social system will depend on conditions which are more complex than the mere existence of objective inequality. Ideology is an important aspect of people's responses to objective disprivilege. There is a consensus in sociology that inequality is rendered acceptable by powerful legitimating cultures. It has been argued that the ideology of equality of opportunity legitimizes existing inequalities because at a 'commonsense' level it suggests that individuals, not society, are to blame for their own failures. Against this position, it has been argued that social actors are far less incorporated in a system by ideologies of legitimation than is conventionally suggested by the sociology of beliefs about the social structure [39]. My own view of the history of social attitudes towards inequality is that it is reluctantly endured by subordinate social groups rather than accepted as normative. In general, I find highly plausible the view expressed by A. J. Gurevich that in the Middle Ages

> the need for inner reconciliation with the demands of their religion was keenly felt among the nobility whose public behaviour was in such glaring contrast with these demands. Less exalted strata of society, drew some moral satisfaction, no doubt, from the spectacle of their social betters doing penitence because they felt less certain of salvation than the poor. [40]

The history of peasant opposition to feudal privilege does not suggest a *normative* commitment to the legitimacy of social gradations based on descent. I draw the same conclusion from contemporary social surveys of the attitudes of workers to existing patterns of social inequality within the industrial societies.

My argument has been that it is reasonable to expect people to accept a certain amount of social inequality under conditions where social mobility is subjectively and objectively possible. Thus, present inequality might be tolerable in the anticipation of future improvement and mobility. We need to enquire more precisely, however, into what is meant by 'acceptance' of social inequality. The argument of this study as a whole is that people rarely accept social inequality as legitimate and just; rather their approach to social life is one of pragmatic acceptance. The position is that people have a sharp consciousness of justice and injustice; consequently they do not give legitimate authority ot social inequalities but are forced pragmatically to accept a status quo which often they cannot significantly change and where realistic alternatives may well be lacking.

The notion that inequality is not given legitimacy follows from a series of arguments originally laid out in *The Dominant Ideology Thesis*. A number of important surveys in Britain in the 1970s showed that working-class people did not accept the existing distribution of wealth as just and fair, nor did they regard the distribution of income as a complete reflection of talent and skill among the managerial and professional classes [41]. Furthermore, a number of comparative enquiries into working-class attitudes towards the justness of the capitalist system would also support the conclusion that subordinates pragmatically accept their circumstances rather than investing these with a normative significance [42]. The sense of an injustice in terms of wage levels is commonly expressed through levels of industrial disputation and conflict, reflecting an underlying rejection of the distribution of wealth in industrial capitalist societies. However, these forms of industrial conflict may also be compensated by rising real standards of living which were achieved in the immediate post-war period in the majority of industrial societies. One can argue that regardless of the sense of injustice, high levels of consumption in capitalist society may also induce a certain pragmatic acceptance of the social structure [43].

Within a comparative perspective, however, British workers are in general regarded as far less radical and class conscious than other sectors of the European working class. When British are compared with French workers there is common agreement between these groups that capitalist society is characterized by inequality, limited forms of upward mobility, substantial features of class closure and limited access to desired social resources. However, there are substantial differences in their attitudes toward these circumstances. French workers exhibit massive alienation form the political system in France and considerable class resentment against their superiors. Furthermore, French workers adopt more fundamental proposals for changing these circumstances via radical and revolutionary activity. By contrast, British workers tend to be pacific and resigned, exhibiting considerable fatalism towards the existence of inequality and measures for reducing such inequality. These differences in the acceptance of inequality are related to such factors as the presence of collective bargaining, the institutionalization of industrial conflict, the attitude of management towards workers, the presence of radical trade unionism and the development of political alternatives through the presence of left-wing political parties [46].

The roots of the French radical tradition and the stability of class relations in Britain may be traced back to the consequences of the First World War for the social structure and government of various European societies. A variety of writers have noted that warfare in the twentieth century has had a profound impact on the social conditions and attitudes of the working class and more widely on the whole set of institutions which constitutes Western industrial democracy [47]. Warfare in the twentieth century brought about a profound increase in state intervention not only in the economy but in society as a whole, creating the circumstances for massive political transformation of the methods of government and administration. Secondly, large-scale mobilization for war brought about a transformation of social attitudes towards customary forms of organization and behaviour. Thirdly, war on a massive scale made plain the role and importance of large-scale collective cooperation and participation in the war effort. Finally, recruitment to the army demonstrated very significant levels of inequality in health within the population and reinforced the idea that the male working-class population was too ill to provide the basis for an effective and healthy fighting force [48].

In the First World War, the devastation brought about in France was much greater than that experienced in Britain and the loss of working-class males created a pool of resentment which was not experienced in other European societies. Furthermore, the French authorities proved inept, not only during, but more importantly after the War, since they failed to bring about any important social reforms which would have ameliorated or transformed the sense of resentment which was characteristic of the French working class. Class antagonism was intensified after the War as a consequence of the intransigence of the French capitalist class and government. The difference in British and French radicalism may as a consequence be seen as the outcome of differences in long-term social and political experience under conditions of industrialization and mass warfare.

SUMMARY

The problem of inequality in modern societies therefore comes back to a complex relationship between politics and economics. Although people are more equal socially than they were as a consequence of modern legislative change, there is also the continuity of basic inequality in terms of prestige, wealth and power. There is a contradiction between the political system in democracies which is based upon public principles of impartiality, fairness and open government and the continuing inequality, especially in economic terms, associated with a capitalist economic base. Capitalist societies are progressive in the sense that their productive base is grounded in the need for free labour, free markets and open access to commodities via modern means of hire purchase, while also generating massive inequality in the distribution of wealth both as a consequence of inheritance through the family and personal achievement in the occupational structure. Modern democracies tend to be relatively incoherent because of this conflict between political equality and economic inequality which modern citizenship has brought about. At an individual level people experience a society which is economically unequal, while being bombarded by political slogans suggesting that democracies are in fact open, free and equal, especially at the level of opportunity. Because governments are dependent upon a popular electoral support, they cannot ignore the demand for welfare and redistribution, but they also have to pay attention to the economic requirements of a free capitalist economy. The problem for capitalist democracies is how to combine competition with welfare [49]. The difficulty with so-called distributive justice is that there has to be an economic surplus to distribute in order to bring about an improvement in the standard of living of the majority of the population. The majority of arguments in favour of economic redistribution do not unfortunately provide an explanation of how high levels of economic growth are to be sustained.

The conditions for capitalist social development are fractured around the contradictions between the legal/political component and the consumption/welfare component. The degree of tolerance which people will exhibit towards a social system based upon fundamental inequality will be a function of these two separate dimensions, that is the combination of political autonomy and economic welfare. In this chapter I have suggested that individuals may be prepared to trade off one component against another. Individuals may be willing to accept social inequalities where there is relatively high consumption and open access to positions which are characterized by high esteem. Furthermore, they may be willing to accept poor economic circumstances where the political system remains relatively open, fair and impartial. The problems for modern national governments, given the internationalization of economic relations, is that it is difficult to develop political programs in a modern democracy where the political and economic components of citizenship can be maintained simultaneously. Capitalist societies are incoherent in that there are major disjunctions between the political and economic processes, but these societies continue because they have managed a consensus in the middle of the political continuum where sufficient socio-economic rewards have been available to the mass of the population. It is for this reason that the strong economic decline of major industrial societies in the early 1980s has presented such a major political problem. Social inequality is inevitable but whether or not it is acceptable will depend upon a range of associated circumstances (such as levels of consumption, social mobility and the impartiality of administration and government). Citizenship may abate the inequalities of class but reformist governments have never been able to remove inequality, especially inequality of income. Inequality of outcome, however, has been made tolerable as a consequence of a variety of institutions which have in the post-war period promoted equality of opportunity.

REFERENCES

[1] Antony Flew, 'The procrustean ideal: libertarians v. egalitarians', *Encounter*, **50**(3), 1978, pp. 70–79.

[2] R. Dahrendorf, 'Liberty and equality, reflections of a sociologist on a classical theme of politics' in *Essays in the Theory of Society*, London, Routledge & Kegan Paul, 1968, pp. 179–214.

[3] G. Markus, *Marxism and Anthropology*, Assen, van Gorcum, 1978, pp. 47–48.

[4] R. Terrill, *R. H. Tawney and his Times*, Cambridge, Mass., Harvard University Press, 1973.

[5] M. Young, *The Rise of the Meritocracy*, London, Thames & Hudson, 1958.

[6] P. Bourdieu, 'Cultural reproduction and social reproduction', in R. Brown (ed.) *Knowledge, Education and Cultural Change*, London, Tavistock, 1973, pp. 71–112.

[7] W. Letwin (ed.), *Against Equality, readings on economic and social policy*, London, Macmillan, 1983.

[8] L. Schapiro, *Totalitarianism*, London, The Pall Mall Press, 1972.

[9] R. Dahrendorf, op. cit., p. 212.

[10] T. Parsons, 'An analytical approach to the theory of social stratification', *American Journal of Sociology*, **45**, 1970, pp. 841–862. K. Davis and W. E. Moore, 'Some principles of stratification', *American Sociological Review*, **10**, 1945, pp. 242–249.

[11] G. A. Huaco, 'The functionalist theory of stratification: two decades of controversy', *Inquiry*, **9**, 1966, pp. 215–240. M. M. Tumin (ed.), *Readings on Social Stratification*, Englewood Cliffs, N. J., Prentice-Hall, 1970.

[12] D. Wrong, *Skeptical Sociology*, London, Heinemann Educational Books, 1977.

[13] S. Hill, *Competition and Control at Work, the new industrial sociology*, London, Heinemann, 1981.

[14] F. F. Piven and R. A. Coward, *Regulating the Poor*, New York, Pantheon Books, 1971.

[15] P. Spicker, *Stigma and Social Welfare*, Beckenham, Croom Helm, 1984, and C. I. Waxman, *The Stigma of Poverty*, New York, Pergamon Press, 1977.

[16] H. J. Gans, *More Equality*, New York, Vintage Books, 1968.

[17] J. H. Turner and C. Starnes, *Inequality, privilege and poverty in America*, Santa Monica, California, Goodyear, 1976.

[18] K. V. Friedman, *Legitimation of Social Rights and the Western*

Welfare State, a Weberian perspective, Chapel Hill, University of North Carolina Press, 1981.

[19] J. Rawls, *A Theory of Justice*, Oxford, Oxford University Press, 1971, p. 302.

[20] D. F. Thompson, *The Democratic Citizen, social science and democratic theory in the twentieth century*, Cambridge, Cambridge University Press, 1970, pp. 153–155.

[21] A. B. Atkinson, *The Economics of Inequality*, Oxford, Clarendon Press, 1975, pp. 51–53.

[22] J. M. Maravall, 'The limits of reformism: parliamentary socialism and the Marxist theory of the state', *British Journal of Sociology*, **30**(3), 1979, pp. 267–290.

[23] D. V. Glass (ed.), *Social Mobility in Britain*, London, Routledge & Kegan Paul, 1954.

[24] J. Westergaard and H. Resler, *Class in a Capitalist Society, a study of contemporary Britain*, London, Heinemann, 1975.

[25] J. H. Goldthorpe, *Social Mobility and Class Structure in Modern Britain*, Oxford, Clarendon Press, 1980.

[26] J. H. Goldthorpe, 'On the service class, its formation and future' in A. Giddens and G. Mackenzie (eds.), *Social Class and the Division of Labour*, Cambridge, Cambridge University Press, 1982, pp. 162–185.

[27] A. Heath, *Social Mobility*, London, Fontana, 1981.

[28] J. W. B. Douglas, *The Home and the School, a study of ability and attainment in the Primary School*, London, MacGibbon & Kee, 1964.

[29] M. Hammersley and P. Woods (eds.), *The Process of School, a sociological reader*, London, Routledge & Kegan Paul, 1976.

[30] B. B. Bernstein, *Class, codes and Control*, London, Routledge & Kegan Paul, 3 vols., 1971, 1973 and 1975.

[31] R. W. Connell, D. J. Ashenden, S. Kessler and G. W. Dowsett, *Making the Difference, schools, families and social division*, Sydney, Allen & Unwin, 1982; W. Labov, 'The logic of non-standard English' in P. P. Giglioli (ed.), *Language and Social Context*, Harmondsworth, Penguin Books, 1972, pp. 179–215.

[32] R. Boudon, *Education, Opportunity and Social Inequality*, New York, John Wiley, 1974.

[33] M. F. D. Young (ed.), *Knowledge and Control*, London, Collier-Macmillan, 1971.

[34] A. H. Halsey, *Change in British Society*, Oxford, Oxford University Press, 1978, p. 130.

[35] W. L. Guttsman, *The British Political Elite*, London, Heinemann, 1963.

[36] R. K. Kelsall, *Higher Civil Servants in Britain*, London, Routledge & Kegan Paul, 1955.

[37] J. Higley, D. Deacon and Don Smart (in collaboration with R. G. Cushing, G. Moore and J. Pakulski), *Elites in Australia*, London, Routledge & Kegan Paul, 1979, p. 87.

[38] A. Shostak, J. van Til and S. van Til, *Privilege in America: an end to inequality?* Englewood Cliffs, N. J., Prentice-Hall, 1973.

[39] J. R. Kluegel and E. R. Smith, 'Beliefs about stratification', *Annual review of Sociology*, 7, 1981, pp. 29–56.

[40] A. J. Gurevich, *Categories of Medieval Culture*, London, Routledge & Kegan Paul, 1984, p. 271.

[41] H. F. Moorhouse, 'The political incorporation of the British working class: an interpretation', *Sociology*, 7(3), 1973, pp. 341–359; H. F. Moorhouse and C. Chamberlain, 'Lower class attitudes to property', *Sociology*, 8(3), 1974, pp. 387–405.

[42] C. Chamberlain, *Class Consciousness in Australia*, Sydney, Allen and Unwin, 1983; H. F. Moorhouse, 'American automobiles and workers' dreams', *The Sociological Review*, 31(3), 1983, pp. 403–426.

[43] D. Rose, C. Vogler, G. Marshall and H. Newby, 'Economic restructuring: the British Experience', *Annuals of the American Academy of Political and Social Science*, 475, 1984, pp. 137–157.

[44] W. G. Runciman, *Relative Deprivation and Social Justice, a study of attitudes to social inequality in twentieth century England*, London, Routledge & Kegan Paul, 1966.

[45] R. Scase, 'Conceptions of the class structure and political ideology: some observations on attitudes in England and Sweden' in F. Parkin (ed.), *The Social Analysis of Class Structure*, London, Tavistock, 1974, pp. 149–177.

[46] D. Gallie, *Social Inequality and Class Radicalism in France and Britain*, Cambridge, Cambridge University Press, 1983; S. Lash, *The Militant Worker, class and radicalism in France and America*, London, Heinemann, 1984.

[47] A. Marwick, *The Deluge: British Society and the First World War*, London, 1965; G. Therborn, 'The rule of capital and the rise of democracy', *New Left Review*, No. 103, pp. 3–41. R. Titmus, *Essays on 'The Welfare State'*, London, Unwin University Books, 1958, Ch. 4; J. Urry, *The Anatomy of Capitalist Society, the economy, civil society and the state*, London, Macmillan, 1981, pp. 147ff.

[48] B. S. Turner, 'The government of the body: medical regimens and the rationalisation of diet', *British Journal of Sociology*, 33(2), 1982, pp. 254–269.

[49] T. Scitovsky, *Welfare and Competition*, Homewood, Illinois, Richard

D. Irwin Inc., 1971; T. Scitovsky, *Papers on Welfare and Growth*, Stanford, California, Stanford University Press, 1964.

3

Social Stratification

MARX, CLASS AND INEQUALITY

The social philosophy of equality commonly starts with the problem of the individual in society by asking questions about natural endowment in relation to personal achievement. The social philosophy of equality and equity tends therefore to concentrate analysis on separate individuals. Although sociologists are clearly interested in the philosophical debate on equality, they discuss inequality and equality within a different language and from a different perspective. The sociologist is less concerned with the nature of inequality as such and more concerned with the explanation of inequality and its social consequences. Sociology consequently tends to be descriptive rather than prescriptive. Furthermore sociology attempts to analyse inequality as a fundamental feature of the structure of societies rather than of the character of persons. For sociology, inequality is a set of relations characterizing social groups, social strata and social classes; the inequality of the individuals is an outcome of their social location within the social structure.

In approaching the analysis of social stratification, contemporary sociology continues to be largely dominated by the influence of Marx and Weber. Marx defined class in terms of the relation of people to the ownership of capital and the means of production. In capitalism there is an expropriation of direct production and the creation of a social class of manual workers who cannot produce on their own account without the intervention of the capitalist. There is a concentration of exclusive possession of the means of production in the hands of a capitalist class which exploits the worker in order to realize profit on investment. In this situation the distinguishing feature of capitalism is the development of labour power as a commodity [1]. The result is a dichotomous division in the social structure where there are two main classes in capitalism, namely the bourgeoisie and proletariat defined by their non-ownership of the means of production. In more simple language, the working clas is forced to sell its labour power in return for a wage to a capitalist class which owns the means of production and which exists as a consequence of profit extracted from the productive process. This picture of the class system of capitalism was complicated in Marx's own sociology by his reference to the petty bourgeoisie who were small-scale, self-employed members of a middle class. Furthermore Marx also identified a lumpen-proletariat composed of thieves, vagabonds and the destitute rejects of early capitalism. Marx also recognized the importance and continuity of the traditional peasantry in French society. Although these traditional and quasi-classes might appear to contradict Marx's dichotomous model of class, they are not necessarily problematic if we remember that Marx was interested in historical formations and transformations of class. Marx often spoke of an inherent trend of pauperization and polarization of classes in capitalism whereby, over time, two main classes would emerge in an antagonistic relationship. This led Marx to refer to classes-in-themselves and classes-for-themselves. By this distinction, Marx attempted to give recognition to the fact that through political and economic struggle the working class gained increasing consciousness of its position and interests in capitalist society.

The implication of Marx's analysis for this discussion of equality is that in the Marxist scheme of sociology inequality is not the outcome of personal defects or moral shortcomings. Inequality is not signficantly an attribute of individuals but a characteristic of society as a whole. Individuals are forced into social roles which are structured socially by relations which ar inherently unequal; individuals are in this sense forced to be unequal. Marx rejected what he took to be the ideology of the bourgeoisie, namely that inequality is the effect of moral character especially such characteristics as laziness and thrift. For Marx prosperity and personal acheivement in capitalism could not be understood in terms of a 'rags to riches mythology'. For Marx the virtues of the spirit of capitalism (hard work, diligence and frugality) could never bring about a radical transformation of the structure of capitalism which by its very nature distributed rewards unequally between social classes which existed independently of the will and wishes of the individuals who existed in capitalism.

Although Marx provided a devastating critique of exploitation in capitalism, his view of history also contains a perspective on social development in which capitalism had a progressive role. For Marx, capitalism by its very revolutionary nature undermined the conventions and traditions of pre-modern society, liquidating the hierarchical structures of the estate system in feudalism. Within a longer historical perspective, capitalism was progressive by comparison with slavery where the individual lacked any personal liberty and was merely an instrument of production. Similarly Marx criticized the vegetative traditionalism of feudal society, rejecting as romantic any glorification of village life. For Marx, the peasant lacked social consciousness and did not provide a radical opposition to traditional social structures. It was only under capitalism that a radical transformation of tradition could be brought about and history constructed in a way which would promote a revolutionary conception of social equality.

In this historical perspective, Marx saw the capitalist mode of production as progressive. While it exploited the worker and the peasant, capitalism liquidated the hierarchical structures of caste and estate which characterized Asiatic society and feudalism. Capitalism destroyed tribalism, patriarchy and the old village system of self-sufficient production. The relations between individuals were no longer structured by descent and blood relations; capitalism simplified personal relations by reducing them to a cash nexus which at one level introduced a radical egalitarian relationship [2]. People were now to be evaluated in simple cash terms, that is in terms of what they could produce and consume. Individuals were treated in terms of a new criterion of monetary value rather than in terms of traditional status and prestige. The worker was 'free' to sell his or her labour on the market for whatever price that labour could realize. The worker was 'free' from the traditional constraints of feudalism and patriarchy. This freedom in economic terms resulted, however, in a paradoxical inequality in terms of class relations. The worker was 'free' to sell labour power to the capitalist and the alternative to this was starvation. The working class was consequently controlled by the 'dull compulsion of everyday relations' rather than by ideology, religion or traditional culture, because the worker is forced to work to eat.

In capitalist society, social relations are dominated by what Marx called the cash nexus where the whole of life becomes the subject of money transactions and economic calculation. Within the cash nexus all services and all things can be reduced to a mere commodity. In Marx's sociology, social life is dominated by exchange values rather than by use values. In capitalism people do not produce things for their own use, but for exchange with other commodities in the market place. Capitalism as a result has a complex character in Marxist theory since it is both liberating (from the restrictions of feudal society) and exploitative (in terms of the extraction of labour power from workers in an unequal class relationship). For Marx, it was only with the development of socialism that the problem of human equality and human needs could be fully satisfied.

Although Marx and Engels refrained from providing a detailed account of socialism on the grounds that socialism had to be created through working-class struggle, they nevertheless held a clear idea of how socialism would operate to resolve the typical problems of bourgeois society, namely the issues of individual freedom, social equality and the satisfaction of needs. In what Marx called 'the higher stage of communist society' the institution of private property and class conflicts would disappear and with the disappearance of these social conflicts the state would wither away, thereby obliterating the economic and political inequalities which characterize capitalism. Socialism was simply a stage on the road to full communist principles in which, according to F. Engels,

> instead of generating misery, over-production will reach beyond elementary requirements of society to assure the satisfaction of the needs of all; it will create new needs and at the same time the means of satisfying them . . . this development of industry will make available to society a mass of products sufficient to satisfy the needs of all . . . . . the division of society into different mutually hostile classes will thus become unnecessary. Indeed it will not only be unnecessary, but irreconcilable with the new social order. [3]

Corresponding to the two stages of post-revolutionary society (socialism and communism), Marxist theory distinguished two kinds of equality. In the first phase of social reconstruction the principle is that 'from each according to his abilities, to each according to the amount of work performed'. This principle of redistribution would not achieve full or just equality, because the society in transition would still retain elements of capitalist conditions. However, under communism the principle would obtain that 'from each according to his abilities, to each according to his needs'. Only under a fully communist regime would there be full equality of treatment for unequal human beings with all their diversity of unequal needs. Under communism the constant striving for individual possession would disappear since society would guarantee a sufficient livelihood for everyone and there would be no longer significant hierarchies of power, prestige and esteem. Achievement motivation and acquisitiveness are not, in Marxism, universal features of human nature, but the specific products of given historical circumstances. In Marxist theory the objective of communist equality and the full satisfaction of need is not utopian but a realistic expectation, given the transformation of social relations which would be brought about by a new mode of production [4].

In attempting a critique of Marx's view of class, sociologists have been typically less concerned with the problems of equality, social needs and individuals in communism and more concerned with a direct critique of Marx's analysis of stratification. In presenting an alternative to Marx's sociology of class, sociologists have frequently turned to the work of Weber and especially to the distinction between class, status and party. Weber defined social classes, status groups and political parties as three distinct dimensions of power within a community, but in practice we allocate relatively little importance to the analysis of political parties in this sociology of social stratification. In this discussion I shall therefore concentrate mainly on the question of Weber's views on social classes and status groups.

WEBER, POWER AND INEQUALITY

Within German society the word for class (*klasse*) was a term used to designate the bourgeoisie and proletariat whereas the word for estates (*stände*) referred to traditional status groups such as the nobility, professions and craftsmen. The development of white collar workers was referred to by the term *mittelstande*. Weber utilized this term to designate status group (*stand*) referring to all of those who occupied a similar status situation within the social structure. A status situation referred to the component of the life of people which is determined by a specific social estimation of honour. The importance of Weber's view was his emphasis on status groups as actual communities characterized by a common lifestyle and pattern of consumption. Status groups had a common lifestyle which they protected by various strategies of social closure designed to exclude competitors and to ensure a monopoly over a particular status within the community.

Weber distinguished two types of classes, namely ownership classes and acquisition classes. The property class is determined by the economic differentiation of property holding, whereas an acquisition class is significantly determined by the opportunity for exploiting services within the market [5]. In summary, Weber treated classes as complex groups whose opportunities and life-chances with respect to the market were very similar.

There are a number of important differences between Marx and Weber with respect to the analysis of social class. Weber's sociology of stratification places emphasis on distribution, consumption and the market, whereas Marxist theories place greater emphasis on production and relations of production. One consequence of this is that Weber's model identifies a plurality of classes rather than a two-class division of the stratification system. Given Weber's emphasis on life-chances in relation to the market, it is not possible to provide a clear means of distinguishing one class from another and furthermore the distribution of life-chances forms a continuum without obvious breaks [6]. Weber's treatment of stratification also suggested that differences in power and prestige cannot be reduced to

differences in property and economic wealth. It follows that for Weber
social conflict is never simply class conflict but involves an intense struggle
between classes, status groups and parties for the monopolization of
privileges and resources with respect to both the market and the system of
production. In Weber's view, social inequality and social conflict were
never simply economic phenomena resulting from a particular mode of
production. Social inequality between classes and status groups was endemic to society as such and as a result Weber did not see the distinction
between socialism and capitalism as sociologically significant. Rather
Weber emphasized the continuity between these types of society in terms of
the continuity of bureaucracy. In Weber's sociology of modern society, the
process of rationalization brought about an increasing dominance of
bureaucracy over the individual and, since socialism would be a planned
society, this would bring about an increasing domination of society by
bureaucratic elites.

Weber's analysis of social stratification has often been criticized from
Marxist standpoints because it cannot clearly identify the boundaries of
social classes and is a descriptive account of social division rather than an
analytical theory of relations of inequality. From a Marxist perspective,
Weber's theory deals with surface phenomena rather than their underlying
causes. In recent sociology, however, there has been less emphasis on the
differences between Marx and Weber and a greater appreciation of their
convergence [7]. Another feature of modern interpretation of Weber is the
emphasis given to the influence of the German philospher F. Nietzsche
since both writers placed great emphasis on the historical importance of
inter-group conflicts and the theme of resentment in human relations [8].
Like Nietzsche, Weber saw human history as the constant oscillation of in-
group and out-group conflict which was ceaseless and gave rise to legitimating ideologies which masked the true role of violence and resentment in
human affairs. In his sociology of religion, Weber typically saw religious
views as the expression of privileged and disprivileged social strata within
the community. While the privileged classes rarely had the need for a
doctrine of salvation, for disprivileged groups religion both compensated
for their deprivation and gave a sublimated expression of their resentment
[9]. Weber saw the conflict between Judaism and the wider gentile environment as a conflict between a pariah people and the host community, a
conflict defined religiously in terms of a division between purity and
impurity. In Weber's political sociology, social life is seen as the ceaseless
struggle for scarce resources between social groups organized to retain or
usurp monopolistic control over distribution. Whereas social classes were
heterogeneous and fissiparous, social status groups were coherent collecti-
vities organized to exert control and conflict in the market place and in the

arena of cultural resources. Status groups have a strong sense of their cultural identity and are mobilized more readily than social classes to pursue distinctive ends.

Weber saw status group conflicts as typical of societies in which the production and distribution of consumption goods was relatively stable, whereas economic class conflict was more common in societies undergoing rapid and violent technological and economic transformation. Where economic stratification is in decline, status conflict and status stratification will be exaggerated and enhanced. In addition there is the implication in Weber's sociology that since status groups emerged both within and without social classes, status group identity will undermine and weaken the sense of class membership and class consciousness. It follows that under the stable conditions of a communist or socialist society, there would be an exaggerated power conflict over lifestyles, consumption goods and prestige. The disappearance of economic class would increase the inequalities of status and prestige within a society. Weber as a consequence saw the struggle around prestige and status in terms of the strategy of social closure and usurpation as universal in human societies.

Social groups attempt to exclude others in order to maintain and improve their control over scarce resources. The practice of social closure is well illustrated in the conflicts surrounding the purity of the caste system where dominant castes attempt to preserve the purity of their position via ritual means and sub-groups attempting to improve their position in the caste system imitate the practices of groups above them through a process known as sanskritization [10].

In the so-called leisure class, status differences are expressed in terms of conspicuous consumption and conspicuous waste whereby an elite sets itself off socially from its competitors by display and exaggerated lifestyles giving emphasis to leisure and ease [11]. By contrast, the nouveau riche attempts to penetrate the leisure class by inter-marriage, by educational attainment and by aping the behaviour and standards of superiors. The status structure of modern society can be conceptualized in terms of an infinite range of social groups attempting to maintain their position by exclusion and to improve their position by usurpation. In particular, credentialism and the diploma disease become crucial features of social advancement and social prestige in a society characterized by universalism and achievement norms [12].

For Weber all human societies are characterized by inequality, because societies are based upon a struggle between groups and individuals over scarce resources. In Weber's sociology, it is power which is the main dimension of inequality, but this dimension can be expressed in a variety of ways. The principal cleavage in Weber's discussion of social structure and inequality is between social class and social status groups. Status groups are involved in a ceaseless struggle to maintain their social standing with respect to competitors and to improve their position relative to those in superior positions. In socialist societies inequality will continue since, while economic class differences may decline or disappear, there will be an intense struggle around status and prestige especially within the party bureaucracy. The cash nexus in Marx is replaced in Weber by a power nexus and bureaucratic conflicts may well replace class conflicts. Marx's notion of the alienation of the worker from the means of production is in Weber simply one instance of a process of rationalization, whereby all members of society are separated from the material and mental means of production. The worker is separated from the economic means of production; the soldier is separated from the means of military violence; the intellectual within the university is separated from the intellectual means of production. Alienation in Marx's sense is simply a version or aspect of Weber's more inclusive notion of rationalization.

Weber's emphasis on the power nexus in society gave rise to an interesting paradox with respect to the relationship between inequality and bureaucracy. In Weber's liberalism, the growth of a state bureaucracy brings about a certain levelling within society since citizens are treated on a universalistic basis irrespective of their particular characteristics as people. Since all are treated alike, all in effect become alike. Bureaucratic regulation was for Weber always domination and as a consequence of this domination individual differences were obliterated under the spreading control of the state. Charismatic authority and traditional patterns of rulership were gradually undermined by these new forms of bureaucratric control, and with the decline of charismatic influence there was again a certain equalization of the population brought about by regulation. When Weber came to describe modern society, he typically used the metaphor of an iron cage in which all individuals were treated uniformly under the regulation of bureaucratic administration and control. Weber's sociology is often constructed around mechanistic metaphors and thus he went on to describe human beings inside modern administered society as simply cogs in a machine. Bureaucracy brought about equality but at the cost of individuality and therefore at the cost of difference and individual hierarchy. However, bureaucracy is essentially a hierarchical organization of offices, and while bureaucracy levels society, it also imposes its own hierarchical forms of power and thus asserts new forms of authoritative inequality. While becoming equal as the objects of bureaucracy, we also become unequal in terms of authority and power within these new bureaucratic organizations of the state. Since Weber thought that socialism would simply be another form of regulation and since socialism will impose even more bureaucratic dominance upon mankind, Weber argued that inequalities of power would be common and indeed predominate within socialist society.

In attempting to understand the similarities and differences between Weber and Marx on social stratification, we should bear in mind the types of society they were attempting to describe and understand in their own period. Marx's mature work was conducted with reference to and in the contest of competitive capitalism in Victorian Britain. In that period economic class relations did appear to have the features attributed to them by Marx, namely a certain polarization and pauperization of classes. This dichotomous society organized in terms of opposing economic classes where state involvement in the economic process was minimal was classically described by F. Engels in *The Condition of the Working Class in England in 1844* [13]. For Engels the economic and cultural gap between the capitalist and the working class was so extreme in Victorian England that he referred to these two classes as two separate tribes.

By contrast, Weber was writing in the context of a German society which had been united by Bismarck's government and German capitalism can be described as a capitalism imposed from above, that is a capitalism which depended for its origins on extensive state intervention. In Germany the bourgeois capitalist class was not politically dominant and the working class was politically under-developed in Weber's view. Germany was dominated by a traditional land-owning class of junkers who controlled the political life of the social system. The special features of German society were reflected in Weber's political sociology, where he was especially concerned with the relationship between bureaucracy and leadership [14]. If Marx's sociology was focused on the problem of exploitation especially in economic relations then we can say that Weber's sociology was focused on the problem of domination in capitalist society and thus upon the inequalities of power and authority within society and the state.

In contemporary sociological theories of social stratification and inequality the legacy of Weber and Marx is clearly apparent in the continuing emphasis on class, status and power in principal dimensions of the social structure of modern societies. Although there is an obvious legacy from Weber and Marx, contemporary theories of stratification and inequality are forced to confront a social structure which has changed radically since the nineteenth and early twentieth century.

POVERTY

Under conditions of competitive capitalism, inequality was primarily determined by the cash nexus. Poverty was largely caused by unemployment and unemployment was primarily caused by illness or aging and by structural features of the economic cycle — boom and slump. In the twentieth century the nexus between the employer and the employee has been significantly influenced by state regulation of the market place which has come about at least partly as a consequence of working-class political action through the trade union movement. With the expansion of citizenship rights, the worker is no longer wholly controlled by economic relations. As a consequence inequality and poverty have changed significantly with these structural changes.

It is no longer the case that the worker is faced with a choice between work and starvation. There are many features of the state's intervention in the market place but they would include the following important components. In Britain between 1965 and 1971 there was the development of a Prices and Income Policy which provided the Government with the means to regulate prices of commodities and the wage demands of unions. Of course the wages policy retained important differentials within the work force as an outcome of the political actions of the trade union movement under the Conservative Government of Margaret Thatcher; there was also a shift towards a monetarist approach tp prices and wages; but even under so-called free market conditions, wages are rarely entirely determined by economic processes alone [15]. Furthermore in Britain, with the development of the welfare state there have been a variety of services available to the unemployed, the poor or the sick. In the post-war period the Family Allowance Act (1945) and the Children Act and National Assistance Act (1948) did much to improve the conditions of the poor and the unemployed by offering an institutional buffer to the impact of the market place. Of course these welfare provisions did not mean that poverty had been eliminated and indeed the extent of poverty has been periodically rediscovered by sociological inquiry [16].

In the early work of S. Rowntree, poverty had been calculated on the basis of a fixed notion of the satisfaction of basic necessities [17]. Rowntree attempted to devise an objective measure of the minimum requirements for the maintenance of life by the use of dietary tables, clothing requirements, heating and shelter. These criteria have subsequently been criticized for their inflexibility and for incorporating a set of social conventions about what is 'necessary' for life behind the illusion of a scientific standard [18]. While there is absolute poverty, it is also important to recognize the existence of relative poverty. Although Rowntree's approach to the measurement of poverty was too narrow, his results were important in showing that social circumstances (illness, accident, family size and unemployment during recession) rather than personal failing were the main determinants of poverty. Rowntree identified a 'cycle of poverty' which were alternating periods of deprivation and relative plenty during the life of a worker. A person may drift in and out of poverty at a number of points in his life-cycle depending on marital status, household composition and age. Therefore, inequalities between families will be a function of their particular location in the cycle of poverty.

There have been important changes in the causes of poverty in industrial society. Rowntree's surveys, based on a narrow definition of poverty, showed that, whereas inadequate wages had been the major cause of poverty in Britain between 1899 and 1936, old age was the most significant determinant of poverty in the 1950s. However, on the basis of a more sophisticated criterion of relative poverty, B. Abel-Smith and P. Townsend in *The Poor and The Poorest* found that poverty had not been conquered by the arrival of the welfare state; furthermore, the principal cause of poverty in their re-analysis of Ministry of Labour data was inadequate wages in relation to family size. The conditions associated with poverty have important implications for government policy in terms of wages, tax thresholds and family allowances. For example, one aspect of poverty and inequality in Britain is the poverty trap. In the United Kingdom a number of benefits are means-tested; an increase in income may result in the loss of such benefits (such as rent and rates rebates) with the consequences that an increase in wages will result in a decline of real standards of living. This trap between income and welfare benefit may also deteriorate with inflationary pressures in the economy. The result is that families whose income is close to the tax threshold cannot escape from poverty as a result of individual effort, thrift and good household management. The evaluative principle of equality of opportunity is clearly problematic in relation to the poverty trap, because individual achievement is no solution to this social dilemma. As a minimum, the resolution of the poverty trap would require significant changes in the tax structure of a society, a re-organization of social security, the development of adequate superannuation and a more positive program towards the elimination of relative as opposed to absolute poverty.

Within these general constraints of social provision and income, the demographic structure of the society and the composition of the household become especially prominent in the organization of poverty and inequality. As we have seen there has been an important increase in the contribution of old age as a principal cause of poverty, indicating significant demographic changes and the increasing importance of early retirement. In these demographic terms there has also been an important decline in the significance of large families as a determinant of poverty. Another feature of modern inequality is the importance of the single-parent household in the distribution of welfare benefits and low income. A number of studies in America and Britain have emphasized the role of household structure in the determination of income and other forms of inequality; single-parent households are often excluded from participation in employment and are forced into a dependency upon the state [19]. In Australia a similar situation obtains and in the late 1970s government pensions were the main source of income for 57 per cent of one-parent income units [20].

The third major determinant of inequality is ethnicity and migrant status. Racial discrimination in a number of modern democratic societies is a critical feature in the distribution of incomes. In America in 1972 for example, it was found that the median incomes of non-white families were less than two-thirds of the incomes of white families. Similarly in Australia, migrant status and ethnic identity are significant determinants of income, health and social prestige [21].

The fourth significant determinant of social and economic inequality in contemporary capitalism is gender identity. Women are over-represented in the less skilled, low-status and low-paid jobs while men are concentrated in the highly skilled and professional occupations. Women dominate the catering, cleaning and other personal-service occupations, where they represent approximately 80 per cent of the workforce. Gender inequality is particularly prominent in the professions, where women are concentrated into those occupations which are relatively low in the professional hierarcy. For example, in Britain in 1971, 91 per cent of nurses were female but only 9 per cent of medical consultants were women [22].

SOCIAL DEMOCRACY

The explanation of poverty is necessarily complex. There are broadly speaking three general explanations of the persistence of poverty in industrial society in modern sociology [23]. There is the notion that a subculture of poverty perpetuates poverty by reproducing the values which have emerged historically as a traditional response to poverty. These responses include fatalism, acquiescence and resignation towards the social deprivation of the working class and other subordinate groups. Criticism of the culture of poverty thesis has led to the notion that it is really a series of situational constraints which account for the prevalence and persistence of poverty. The poor are constrained by their environment, including poor housing, low incomes and inadequate education. Against both perspectives, it is claimed these two explanations are addressed to the continuity, not the origins of poverty. Poverty can only be understood within a broader analysis of inequality, that is within an interpretation of social stratification. In terms of the argument of this book, the nature of inequality in a society (and hence the distribution of poverty within the population) will be a function of the relationship between the socio-economic rights of citizenship and the divisive impact of the capitalist market place. In short, it will be a problem of social democracy. We can illustrate this perspective by a brief consideration of the recent history of Swedish social democracy.

In Chapter 1, I argued that the development of a notion of equality as a general social value required the development of universal citizenship. Against an evolutionary view of modernization, it was claimed that social citizenship has been the product of profound and often violent social changes. Three conditions for modern citizenship (in conjunction with a religio-moral view of the universal value of persons) were discussed: class conflict, popular struggles in war-time and migration. The implication of this view is that it requires a dramatic shock to the social structure to bring about a significant shift in the pattern of inequality in society. In his classic study of income inequality in America, C. Jencks came to the conclusion that 'it takes a cataclysm like the Great Depression or World War II to alter the distribution of income significantly. Political shifts, such as the election of a liberal or a conservative President, seem to have quite minor effects, except on the very rich and the very poor' [24]. In Marxist terms, it requires a revolutionary overthrow of the existing system of property relations through the medium of class conflict to achieve a real transformation of the balance of wealth and power in society.

Within this perspective, Sweden is an important case study since it appears to depart from the model of revolutionary politics as the only route to socialism. In modern Swedish economic and political arrangements there has been a major advancement of the working class without a preceding history of class conflict, warfare or disruptive migration. Although Sweden was involved in a number of international conflicts in the eighteenth century, it has not had any significant military conflicts since 1814. The Swedish Social Democratic party was in power from 1932 to 1976 and, after a brief period in opposition, returned to office in September 1982. The Swedish labour force is one of the most highly unionized in the industrial world (around 85 percent). Under socialism a progressive system of social insurance was created, along with state regulation of essential services. There was government support for workers' cooperatives. Measures were also taken to involve workers in the ownership of companies through the creation of wage-earner funds [25]. The socialist government pursued a policy of full employment, removed legal obstacles to public-sector unionization, enhanced the bargaining position of the work force and reduced the employees' dependence on the owners of capital. These changes suggest that there has been a progressive 'decommodification' of labour power in Swedish society which is a distinctively anti-capitalist trend. In terms of social citizenship, this transformation of labour represents the replacement of social democracy by economic democracy.

There are a number of criticisms of this interpretation of recent Swedish history. It can be shown that, despite the electoral successes of socialism and continuous socialist government, there has not been a major transformation of wealth in Sweden. Private wealth continues to be dominant, especially in the industrial sector. In the 1970s, fifteen families and two corporations had predominant ownership in 200 companies, which employed around 50 per cent of the labour force in the private sector [26]. The Wallenberg family controlled 15 per cent of the 280 largest firms in Sweden [27]. Sweden's industrial dynastic families have survived half a century of social democratic legislation without any significant erosion of their dominance in the domestic economy [28]. Public ownership in industry has remained insignificant at about 5 per cent in the 1970s. In short, the Swedish case shows both the strength and the limitations of reformism within a capitalist framework [29]. The defence of reformism must be that the alternatives are either not entirely feasible on sociological grounds or not desirable with respect to moral arguments concerning individual freedoms. Since it is very difficult to eradicate inequality under any set of social circumstances, there are good reasons to press for reform, however limited the likely outcome.

There is however, a more limited lesson to draw from the Swedish experience and that lesson concerns the increasing importance of the external constraints on domestic economies, making reformist objectives difficult to achieve because of adverse international economic trends. Social democratic reforms, where they are successful in achieving the decommodification of labour, must threaten private-sector profitability where the expansion of the welfare state supplies services which are not commodified. Since the Swedish economy has become increasingly subject to international economic forces, these welfare services add to the fiscal crisis of the state in welfare capitalism. The external constraints make a government commitment to full employment difficult to maintain without inflationary pressures undermining the currency. The basic difficulty for modern governments is to achieve control over the economy in the interest of domestic and reformist objectives when economic growth is determined by external processes which cannot be controlled [30]. Reviewing the recent literature on Sweden and reformism, J. Pontusson noted that the internationalization of economic processes has produced an entirely new framework for social reform:

While the Great Depression may be described as a 'crisis of under consumption', and as such lent itself to a reformist political response based on the stimulation of popular consumption, the current crisis first and foremost appears to be a crisis of over-capitalization and insufficient profit margins [31].

In the present context this change of economic circumstances means that even the modest attempt to achieve equality of conditions may be constantly thwarted by unfavourable externalities. While the social quest for greater domestic equality by post-war governments of reconstruction might have been feasible in the 1950s, this cannot be the platform for reformism in the 1980s. The objective conditions of equality are international, because local inequalities, while clearly a product of internal stratification, are tied to macro-processes of economic decline, deindustrialization and dependency.

PARAMETERS OF WELFARE CAPITALISM

My argument has been that the cash nexus which dominated class inequality in the nineteenth century has been modified by the expansion of citizenship, the intervention of the state and the growth of welfare policies under the general framework of Keynesian economics. Despite the growth of the welfare state, the problem of relative deprivation and poverty continue, but many of the determinants of inequality are only indirectly related to economic class. I have suggested that income inequality in particular is closely related to age, household structure, ethnicity and gender, that is, mainly to ascriptive status within the community. Although these dimensions are related to social class, the determinants of inequality are more obviously components of prestige and ascriptive social roles. The emphasis of Marx and Engels on economic class is less relevant in contemporary society than Weber's characterization of the nature of domination and status groups.

The analysis of inequality in modern society requires an emphasis on social conflict and social closure from the perspective of conflict theory rather than from the perspective of either social stratification theory within a functionalist framework or from a Marxist economic class analysis. Weber's conceptualization of society in terms of an endless struggle between classes, status groups and professional associations via the strategies of social closure to mobilize and monopolize the resources of wealth, power and esteem therefore receives considerable vindication in the study of modern inequality.

Those social groups which find it difficult to organize collectively are forced to the margins of society and suffer stigmatization and exclusion. The plight of the aged in modern capitalist society is well illustrated by this process of stigmatization. The process of social aging forces the elderly into a situation of life-cycle dependency and their lack of reciprocity with the wider society brings about a stigmatization of age associated with significant forms of discrimination and victimization [32]. The inability of the aged to form effective political groups to represent their interests has limited their ability to achieve significant improvements in their social and economic position. In general terms we can say that women, the aged and ethnic minority groups suffer a social exclusion which forces them into cultural ghettos and limits their access to the full benefits of egalitarian citizenship.

INEQUALITY AND PRIVILEGE

The discussion of inequality within the framework of sociological theories of stratification has so far concentrated on questions of poverty, deprivation and low esteem. Of course the question of inequality is also closely connected with the nature of privilege. In sociological theory, privilege has been strangely neglected in the major texts on stratification [33]. Inequality is not simply about poverty and deprivation, but also importantly about wealth and privilege. The privilege of the professions for example is maintained by occupational closure which via credentialism and the diploma disease strengthens the occupational privilege of professional groups in the market place and maintains their control over economic and prestige rewards. The professions develop educational entry requirements into their ranks which have relatively little relevance to the actual performance of occupational tasks, but have a great significance with respect to their status and privilege in the wider community. Professionalism has relatively little relationship to systematic bodies of knowledge, but bears a close relationship to occupational dominance and market control via control and the maintenance of professional privileges via recruitment and educational resources [34]. Within the sociology of professions and occupational sociology, the explanation of social inequality would appear to depend heavily on Weber's analysis of social closure, but it depends relatively marginally on Marx's view of economic exploitation and economic social classes.

There have been significant changes in the nature of modern capitalist societies which have rendered problematic many of the initial notions concerning social inequality in the work of Weber and Marx, but Weber's concept of social closure is valuable in understanding inequality in modern welfare capitalism. Inequality, disprivilege and poverty in this type of society continue to be significantly influenced by ascriptive features of social identity. However, the achievement of equal rights presupposes the successful mobilization of social groups to usurp the limitation placed upon their status in society. In part, inequalities of status are closely bound up with important changes in the class structure of modern capitalism. Firstly, there has been a significant decline in the size of the working class. In Britain between 1911 and 1971 the size of the manual worker class fell from 80 to just over 58 per cent of the employed population. Correspondingly there was an increase in higher professionals from 1 to over 3 per cent and lower professionals from 3 to almost 8 per cent of the employed population. There has also been a significant increase in white-collar clerical employment which rose considerably in the first half of the twentieth century with the result that clerks increased from 5 to 14 per cent of the employed population. These changes in the class structure are reflected in a growing level of white-collar unionization and in the relatively static level of manual workers with uinion membership [35]. These changes in the class structure are closely associated with the decline of traditional heavy industry and the growth of computerized production.

There has been considerable de-skilling of the population and changes in the technical nature of work have both reduced the size of the manual working class and increased the size of white-collar employment. Although sociologists like D. Bell had predicted these changes in the class structure as a consequence of the growth of industrial productivity, more recent theories of deindustrialization regard these changes as a consequence of poor economic performance; deindustrialization is thus regarded not as a consequence of economic transformation but of economic decline [36]. With de-skilling and de-industrialization some sociologists have interpreted these changes as constituting the disappearance of the traditional working class [37]. One indicator of British decline and deindustrialization has been the significant growth in unemployment rates in the 1970s. In Britain the official rate of unemployment rose from 6 to 11 per cent between 1979 and 1981 compared to the rise in the United States from 6 to 8 per cent [38]. By 1985 it exceeded 13 per cent in Britain.

The social consequences of deindustrialization for inequality are relatively obvious. The Government family expenditure survey in Britain has shown that in 1983 15 million people were living on the margins of poverty, compared with 11.5 million in 1979. The new unemployed and poor sectors of the population are almost wholly dependent on the state for support because they are either in retirement or permanently unemployed. However, that section of the population which has maintained employment has experienced a significant improvement in their real standard of living in the late 1970s. The division between employment and unemployment is thus a significant feature of income and welfare equality in Britain, but the character of inequality in modern society is in fact far more complex than simply a question of employment and taxation. The new divisions in British society are between north and south, employed and unemployed, those on state benefits and those who are caught in the poverty trap, between men and women, between age groups and finally between different segments of the skilled labour market. A multiplicity of conflicts and dimensions determine the character of social inequality in welfare capitalism, but this complexity is further evidence for the value of Weber's emphasis on status-group conflicts and social closure.

One political consequence of this multidimensional form of inequality is a desubordination of the population in which society becomes characterized by 'continued conflict, antagonistic industrial relations and a climate in which cooperation between the two sides of industry remains as elusive as ever, notwithstanding the objurgations [scoldings (ed.)] of politicians, prelates and princes. Strike action is an habitual feature of such a situation, and episodically assumes the character of major and de-stabilizing confrontations between labour and the state' [39]. Whether or not these separate and isolated forms of conflict over the distribution of wealth will result in more concerted radical political action will depend to some extent on whether inequality is seen to be legitimate and whether the unequal distribution of wealth is in fact a just distribution of limited resources. Commitment to equality of condition as a feasible and desirable social goal will depend a great deal on the ideological effectiveness of the concept of the autonomous moral individual and of individual responsibility. The failure or otherwise of egalitarianism as a social principle will in turn depend on the uncertain future relationship between political democracy and the international economic market.

REFERENCES

[1] A. Cottrell, *Social Classes in Marxist Theory*, London, Routledge & Kegan Paul, 1984.

[2] M. Berman, *All that is Solid Melts into Air, the experience of modernity*, New York, Simon & Schuster, 1982.

[3] F. Engels, *Principles of Communism*, Peking, Foreign Languages Press, 1977, p. 18.

[4] A. Heller, *The Theory of Need in Marx*, London, Allison & Busby, 1974.

[5] M. Weber, *Economy and Society*, 3 vols., New York, Bedminster Press, 1968.

[6] N. Abercrombie and J. Urry, *Capital, Labour and the Middle Classes*, London, Allen & Unwin, 1983.

[7] F. Parkin, *Max Weber*, Chichester, Ellis Horwood, and London, Tavistock, 1982.

[8] B. S. Turner, 'Nietzsche, Weber and the devaluation of politics: the

problem of state legitimacy', *The Sociological Review*, **3**(3), 1982, pp. 367–391.

[9] M. Weber, *The Sociology of Religion*, London, Methuen, 1966.

[10] M. N. Srinivas, *Caste in Modern India*, London, Asia Publishing House, 1962.

[11] T. Veblen, *The Theory of the Leisure Class, an economic study of institutions*, London, Allen & Unwin, 1925.

[12] F. Parkin, *Marxism and Class Theory, a bourgeois critique*, London, Tavistock, 1979; R. Dore *The Diploma Disease*, London, Allen & Unwin, 1976.

[13] F. Engels, *The Condition of the English Working Class in 1844*, London, Allen & Unwin, 1920.

[14] A. Giddens, *Politics and Sociology in the Thought of Max Weber*, London, Macmillan, 1972.

[15] P. Hirst, 'The division of labour, incomes policy and industrial democracy' in A. Giddens and G. Mackenzie (eds.), *Social Class and the Division of Labour*, Cambridge, Cambridge University Press, 1982, pp. 248–264.

[16] B. Abel-Smith and P. Townsend, *The Poor and the Poorest*, Occasional papers on Social Administration, No. 17, Bell & Sons, London, 1965; K. Coates and R. Silburn, *Poverty: the Forgotten Englishmen*, London, Penguin Books, 1970; P. Townsend, *The Social Minority*, London, Allen Lane, 1973; D. Wedderburn (ed.), *Poverty, Inequality and Class Structure*, London, Cambridge University Press, 1973.

[17] S. Rowntree, *Poverty: a Study of Town Life*, London, Macmillan, 1901; *Poverty and Progress*, London, Longmans, 1941; *Poverty and the Welfare State*, London, Longmans, 1951.

[18] P. Townsend, *Poverty in the United Kingdom*, London, Allen Lane, 1979.

[19] A. B. Atkinson, *The Economics of Inequality*, Oxford, Clarendon Press, 1975, Ch. 10.

[20] A. Burns., G. Bottomley and P. Jools (eds.), *The Family in the Modern World*, Sydney, Allen & Unwin, 1983, p. 202.

[21] J. S. Western, *Social Inequality in Australian Society*, Melbourne, Macmillan, 1983; R. A. Wild, *Social Stratification in Australia*, Sydney, Allen & Unwin, 1978.

[22] L. Murgatroyd, 'Gender and occupational stratification', *The Sociological Review*, **30**(4), 1982, pp. 574–602; C. Middleton 'Sexual inequality and stratification theory' in F. Parkin (ed.), *The Social Analysis of the Class Structure*, London, Tavistock, 1974, pp. 179–203.

[23] M. Haralambos, *Sociology, themes and perspectives*, Slough, University Tutorial Press, 1980.

[24] C. Jencks, *Inequality, a reassessment of the effect of family and schooling in America*, New York, Basic Books, 1972, pp. 209–210.

[25] W. Korpi, *The Working Class in Welfare Capitalism, work, unions and politics in Sweden*, London, Routledge & Kegan Paul, 1978; W. Korpi, *The Democratic Class Struggle*, London, Routledge & Kegan Paul, 1983; J. Stephens *The Transition from Capitalism to Socialism*, London, Macmillan, 1979.

[26] R. F. Tomasson, *Sweden, prototype of modern society*, New York, Random House, 1970.

[27] R. Scase (ed.), *Readings in the Swedish Class Structure*, London, Pergamon Press, 1976.

[28] J. Scott, *Corporations, Classes and Capitalism*, London, Hutchinson, 1979.

[29] J. M. Marävall, 'The limits of reformism: parliamentary socialism, and the Marxist theory of the State', *The British Journal of Sociology*, **30**(3), 1979, pp. 267–290.

[30] R. Vernon, *Sovereignty at Bay*, New York, Basic Books, 1971.

[31] J. Pontusson, 'Behind and beyond social democracy in Sweden', *New Left Review*, No. 143, 1984, p. 93.

[32] E. S. Johnson and J. B. Williamson, *Growing Old, the social problems of aging*, New York, Holt, Rinehart & Winston, 1980; A. Walker, 'Dependency and old age', *Social Policy and Administration*, **16**(2), 1982, pp. 115–135; C. Phillipson, *Capitalism and the Construction of Old Age*, London, Macmillan, 1982.

[33] D. Portwood and A. Fielding, 'Privilege and the professional', *The Sociological Review*, **29**(4), 1981, pp. 749–769.

[34] T. J. Johnson, *Professions and Power*, London, Macmillan, 1972; B. S. Turner, 'Knowledge, skill and occupational strategy: the professionalization of paramedical groups', *Community Health Studies*, **9**(1), 1985, pp. 38–47.

[35] R. Price and G. S. Bain, 'Union growth revisited', *British Journal of Industrial Relations*, **14**, 1976, pp. 339–355.

[36] D. Bell, *The Coming of Post-Industrial Society*, London, Heinemann, 1974; F. Blackaby (ed.), *De-industrialisation*, London, Heinemann, 1979.

[37] A. Gorz, *Farewell to the Working Class: an essay on post-industrial Socialism*, London, Pluto, 1982.

[38] N. Harrs, *Of Blood and Guns*, Harmondsworth, Penguin, 1983.

[39] R. Miliband, *Capitalist Democracy in Britain*, Oxford, Oxford University Press, 1982.

4

Ideologies of Inequality

I have suggested that we should as sociologists consider three positions with respect to inequality. The first is that inequality is a universal feature of all human societies since individuals are stratified on a variety of dimensions as a consequence of the very existence of social norms and sanctions. Secondly, it has been argued that resistance to inequality, as a consequence of the sense of fairness, is also endemic and fundamental to all social relations on the basis of the reciprocity which underlies all social reality. Thirdly, I have suggested that inequality is legitimated in society by reference to a variety of ideological systems which attempt to explain the necessity and legitimacy of all forms of inequality. In this chapter I shall consider three systems for legitimizing inequality, namely religious, natural and economic explanations.

Most forms of traditional ideology legitimating inequality between persons have been religious in character, but I shall argue that religion has a typically ambiguous role to play as a legitimation of social and personal inequality. This question of the relationship between religion and inequality has also to be considered in a comparative fashion with respect to the idea that some religious traditions are more committed to the legitimacy of inequality than other religious traditions. It is valuable to consider the problem of religion and inequality within the framework of the sociology of religion of Weber.

RELIGION AND INEQUALITY

Weber's sociology of religion can be seen as a comparative study of the conditions for the emergence of modern society, where modern societies are characterized by the rationalism of their intellectual system, the emphasis on individual autonomy, and the development of a bureaucratic apparatus of social control. In Weber's comparative sociology of religion there is a continuum between those religious systems which promote modernism (Calvinistic Protestantism) and those religious traditions which stand in opposition to the process of modernization (namely, those religious systems which Weber referred to as Asiatic). In Weber's account of Hinduism, Confucianism and Buddhism, we find the argument that Asiatic religions involve the transmission of a special type of knowledge (gnosis) to a cultured elite via a period of training and adherence to ritual which guarantees purity. The religions of Asia were grounded in a religious notion of inequality.

In regard to Hinduism, Weber's argument was that it is impossible to be a Hindu without being a member of a caste and it is impossible to be a member of a caste without being a Hindu. In this sense it can be argued that Hinduism is constituted by the fact of inequality, that is inequality between castes [1]. Weber also saw Confucianism and Buddhism as religious systems grounded in a fundamental inequality between the excellence of the ritualistic experts (the virtuosi) and the lay person who could not fulfil the full demands of the religion. Confucianism in particular was a religion which was developed to meet the courtly requirements of the literati and exhibited extreme disdain towards the lower classes. In general Weber saw religion as the cultural response of specific groups of privileged and disprivileged persons towards the problem of the meaningfulness of their lives [2].

In particular Weber argued that systems of religious belief provided various forms of theodicy, namely religious ideologies which explained the character of injustice in society by reference to some supernatural person or some supernatural reality. This theme of theodicy has been taken up in contemporary sociology of religion by P. L. Berger who has argued that most societies contain two contrasted theodicies, that is a theodicy for the rich and a theodicy for the poor [3]. A theodicy of happiness legitimates the wealth and prestige of privileged classes by suggesting that they are morally and spiritually deserving of their elevated status in this world, which is a mark of their superior spiritual development. A theodicy of suffering explains the misery of the poor by suggesting that their poverty is legitimate as a consequence of sin but that through collective and individual development the poor may inherit the kingdom in the next world. In the view of Berger these theodicies by legitimating inequality and wealth stabilize the social system, but also provide meaning for individuals, thereby minimizing their sense of anomie and dislocation.

In Berger's sociology of religion, Hinduism provided the most clear illustration of a theodicy which legitimizes and provides authority for social inequality as expressed through the caste system. There are three aspects of Hindu doctrine which provide a fundamental legitimization of the system of social strata and these are *dharma*, *karma* and *samsara*. These religious terms have a central role to play in Hinduism where for example *dharma* is a Sanskrit word which at its root means self-subsistence but in a more developed way means a universal law or norm. In terms of caste system each *varna* or caste has its own specific moral code of *dharma* outlining the appropriate behaviour for members of such social groups.

Next, *karma* signifies the consequences of individual and social action, but in the context of caste *karma* means the consequence of behaviour in a previous existence so that one's present social status is seen to be the effect of previous moral action.

Finally, *samsara* means literally 'wandering', but in its religious context refers to the continuous process of birth and death from one life to another in a system of reincarnation.

The combined effect of these three concepts is to explain present social inequality by reference to the moral character of the individual in previous incarnations. The society is consequently not to blame for poverty and wealth since it is the individual who is held entirely responsible for their current social status by reference to the cycle of birth and re-birth. According to the tradition which unites Weber and Berger, the *dharma/samsara/karma* theodicy provides the most total and coherent religious explanation of inequality but also provides a moral justification for this structure based upon massive inequalities of prestige and wealth.

Against the Hindu religion and more generally the Asiatic religions, Weber regarded Christianity as a progressive social doctrine because it was the seed bed for Western notions of individual responsibility, social universalism and equality. Weber argued that Christianity, by placing great emphasis on faith as the basis of a Christian community, undermined the importance of blood and kinship relations in the constitution of traditional societies. That is, the social basis of relationships within the early Christian church was a commitment to the person of Christ (or more indirectly commitment to a system of religious propositions or a creed) rather than a commitment via descent and tribal affiliation to a social leader. One consequence of this development was that the European city was based upon a notion of general citizenship rather than on ties of family and tribe [4]. Within this religious tradition all citizens were equal under the same political institution because they were all equal under the fatherhood of God.

In general all of the so-called Abrahamic faiths (Judaism, Christianity and Islam) had these universalistic features, but in Weber's view it was only in Protestant Christianity that the doctrine of radical equality was developed to its final limit. Protestant Christianity was able to combine together the notion of the individualism of the Christian believer with the doctrine of total equality of all believers [5]. The Christian believer was totally alone before God without the support or help of liturgy and sacraments, but the individual was also radically equal alongside all other individuals since God was absolute and also distant. This Protestant emphasis on individualism has been associated with the emergence of individualistic capitalism and this feature of the Protestant religion is interesting with respect to Protestant attitudes towards inherited wealth.

The Protestant Reformation through the emphasis on ascetism made money 'clean' by undermining many of the traditional ethical controls over wealth, accumulation and consumption. Money which has been acquired through hard work and effort was clean money, and indeed became the symbol or sign of inner-worldy purity and virtue [6]. The existence of inequality of wealth was perfectly acceptable to the Protestant mind, provided that wealth has been acquired through denial and effort. In short. Protestant individualism tended to encourage a moral commitment to the importance of equality of opportunity and a society open to talent. By contrast, the Protestant divines were wholly opposed to inherited wealth on the part of the traditional aristocracy, since this wealth was not necessarily earned by the individual. Protestantism by its rejection of inherited wealth emphasized the importance of individualism, achievement and asceticism, values which have been associated with the origins of modern capitalism.

Within this framework Christianity was significant in promoting the idea of ontological equality and equality of opportunity through the doctrine of the fatherhood of God and the moral emphasis on individual virtue. By contrast, Catholicism was often associated with the notion of a 'great chain of being' [7]. Medieval theodicies were religious explanations of human and social variety, diversity and inequality. The Christian theodicy gave rise eventually to a powerful social metaphor in the history of European philosophy, namely that existence was organized in a great chain of beings. This metaphor argued that all the grades of conscious life in the world from animals to angels were connected to God by an infinite number of links in a chain. The great chain metaphor saw the universe as infinitely rich but each feature of this complex totality was ordered hierarchically. Intelligent sentient life was ranked closer to God than the inanimate world of the lower orders, whereas the spiritual grades of angels and men were closely linked to God. There was no break in this chain so that no feature of reality was finally excluded from contact with God, since the chain was characterized by complete continuity. One vulgar version of this metaphor argued that

> The rich man in his castle,
> The poor man at his gate —
> God made them high and lowly,
> And ordered their estate.

While Hinduism developed a theodicy of caste through the doctrine of *dharma*, Catholic medieval Christianity had a similar view of the justness and appropriateness of social inequality through a variety of metaphors which justified hierarchies of inequality.

While the Abrahamic faiths provided doctrines of radical equality, by giving special importance to the notion of the fatherhood of God, Christianity could also generate quite specific theories of social inequality. One crucial historical problem for Christianity has been the existence of slavery. The same is true for Islam, since Islam was committed to a universalistic faith, but developed through the social institution of slavery which became part of the whole military establishment of Islamic empire [8].

As we have seen sociologists like Weber treated Calvinism as a socially radical doctrine which contributed to the modern demolition of tradition, heirarchy and superstition; but Weber made no commentary on the role of Calvinistic religion in legitimating, or at least accepting, the institution of slavery. While Weber argued that Islam took slavery for granted, it is interesting to consider the role of Calvinism in the Western acceptance of slavery as either a necessary evil or as a perfectly justified and justifiable social relation which offered distinctive economic advantages, especially in the colonies. For example, in the Dutch colonies of the East Indies in the seventeenth and eighteenth centuries, there emerged a distinctive slave-holding society stratified by ethnicity [9]. The racial orders of the East Indies were parallel to those which emerged in New Holland where slavery became a necessary feature of the economy, since it proved impossible to attract free-born Dutchmen to the new colonies in the seventeenth century. With few exceptions the majority of the Reformed clergy felt no theological or moral incompatibility between Christian doctrine and slavery. Indeed since Calvinism came to see the slave as a sinner, slavery was thought to be an appropriate social condition for this inferior race. The Dutch Calvinistic clergy came eventually to describe a slave as dirty, black, lazy and polluted. Slavery was a just punishment for these constitutional sinners and the Dutch colonies developed a fairly rigid ethnic structure of massive inequality [10]. The heritage of these ideologies may clearly be seen in the contemporary crisis of South Africa, where the policy of *Apartheid* has religious justification in the teachings of the Dutch Reformed Church.

Christians saw that they had a mission towards the slaves to convert their souls but this left the institution of slavery unquestioned. This development in Christianity can be seen as an example of the more general problem of the inevitability of stratification in human societies. While Christianity could recognize all human beings as equal before God, this created a normative system from which there could be deviation. This deviance in Christian doctrine is called sin and the existence of sin necessarily creates a hierarchical and unequal social structure, namely a distinction between the sinful and the sinless. The existence of sin as deviance was not simply a question of differentiation only, but more significantly gave rise to a new form of religious stratification between those who were full with the spirit of God and those who were still full with the spirit of Adam. Negro slavery could therefore be justified (despite the commitment to a universalistic notion of salvation) on the grounds that the negro was the living embodiment of human wickedness. Although this characterization of so-called inferior races was closely associated with Calvinism, the same (or at least similar) justification occurred with other branches of Christianity. Of course the liberation of slaves became eventually a specific goal of certain Christian societies, but even in the twentieth century there are still societies where Dutch Calvinism is the ideological basis of the justification of inequality between races — South Africa being the prime example [11].

NATURAL INEQUALITY

With the secularization of industrial capitalist societies, religious legitimation of stratification either through the notion of a great chain of being or through the notion of sin has become less significant socially. The legitimation of racial and economic inequality in the nineteenth and twentieth centuries has often been associated instead with the development of Social Darwinism, biologism or eugenics. In the nineteenth century social theory was significantly influenced by the biological theory of C. Darwin (1809–1882).

While Darwin himself was not necessarily concerned with the development of human societies through the processes of adaptation and evolution, Darwin's ideas on selection in evolutionary development were easily adopted by social philosophers and sociologists, especially by writers like H. Spencer [12]. Social Darwinism was an application of the notion of evolution and natural selection to the historical growth of human society which gave a special significance to the notion of the 'survival of the fittest'. While departing significantly from Darwin's own views on biology, Social Darwinism became popular especially in America towards the end of the nineteenth century when it was used as an explanation for imperialism and racism. Social Darwinists argued that there were underlying and irresistible biological forces acting on human societies which were like the forces of nature acting upon animal and plant communities. Social Darwinism thus has a strong attraction for a society committed to a scientific ideology of truth and excellence. These social forces produced evolutionary progress through endless conflict, adaptation and survival, so that the best qualified and most intelligent life forms emerge as predominant in the evolutionary process. The best-adapted social groups survived this endless conflict between social groups and their environment with the result that the evolutionary capacity of society as a whole was improved through a process of differentiation and integration.

There was a natural relationship between the Social Darwinistic emphasis on the conflict between groups and the character of early competitive capitalism as a society based upon the conflict between the worker and the employer. In North America, Social Darwinism had a special appeal, being used to justify laissez-faire social policies which argued that the state should not interfere in social relations since social relations would develop and evolve most appropriately through unregulated conflict. For Social Darwinists, the natural superiority of the white races over other racial groups was evidence of the validity of Darwinistic notions of the survival of the fittest and any attempt to influence or control this evolutionary logic would necessarily end in biological disaster. The black races were socially inferior as a consequence of the logic of nature and any attempt to interbreed with these races would undermine the natural superiority of the white races [13].

In Social Darwinism, eugenics and biologism, we have a social ideology which explains and legitimates race relations and social inequality generally as the inevitable outcome of fixed laws of natural development and selection; furthermore, these so-called natural laws of development have the beneficial consequence of preserving the human species and promoting the successful evolution of those most adept, fitted and intelligent. All policies designed to change or ameliorate these circumstances were regarded as misguided, since they would contribute to a decline of the stock of those social groups which were the strongest, the fittest and the most intelligent.

These Darwinistic theories legitimating inequality were often combined with fascist theories of human inequality to produce a political outlook justifying policies of racial purification and extermination. The development of the notion of racial determination owed a great deal to the work of A. de Gobineau who published *Essay on the Inequality of the Human Races* (1853–1855) and H. S. Chamberlain who was the author of *Foundations of the Nineteenth Century* (1899). The theories of Gobineau and Chamberlain laid much of the basis for what became subsequently Nazism insofar as the Nazi ideology was grounded in an anti-semitic and racist position. Nazism shared many of the general characteristics of fascism which was committed to the notion that the Aryan race was racially superior to other races, to a position of anti-semitism and to the notion of the superiority of German military power.

Social Darwinism has been the subject of considerable criticism in social theory [14]. One paradox was that Spencer's commitment to laissez-faire politics was developed in a period when the state was increasingly intervening in the social organization of the industrial societies. Evolutionary theory has been the subject of massive critical opposition and the notion that biology might have any contribution to the development of sociological thought has also been the topic of considerable critical review [15]. The basic criticism of these biological deterministic arguments is that it is not clear that the concept of race has any valid scientific status and furthermore it is far from evident that biological processes and structures have any bearing on social reality apart from providing a metaphorical language of social phenomena. Despite these intellectual criticisms of Darwinism and evolutionary, racist ideology clearly plays a significant part in continuing to legitimate racial inequality in modern industrial societies. In contemporary Singapore, for example there is widespread anxiety on the part of the political authorities that the low level of fertility among the middle class will reduce the quality of the stock of people who constitute Singaporian society.

POLITICAL ECONOMY

I have considered two ideological traditions which provide a justification for social inequality (the religious tradition and the social philosophy of Social Darwinism). I have suggested that the process of secularization diminished the significance of religious ideologies of inequality which were in the nineteenth century replaced by a set of doctrines emerging from Darwin's biological views on evolution. There is a third tradition which can justify inequality which is predominantly secular and closely associated with the emergence of industrial capitalism. This third view on inequality is associated with utilitarianism and with the classical political economy of modern capitalism. This view of economic struggle is also fundamentally associated with the notion of possessive individualism, achievement and initiative. The economic doctrine of inequality associated with utilitarianism is fundamental to the general culture of capitalist society. It is difficult to distinguish between political theories of inequality and the classical economic analysis of inequality arising from the market place. In political terms, the notion of possessive individualism assumes inequality as part of the very definition of society, that is possessive market society. As C. B. Macpherson has noted in his classic study of Hobbes and Locke, possessive society was defined as one in which all individuals seek to maximize utilities rationally but some individuals desire a greater level of utilities than they have and furthermore some individuals have more energy, skill or possessions, than other persons in the market place [16].

For example, in Locke's treatment of property and value, he argued that a man's labour is his own property and that the property owner should have the benefits of the value arising from their property. However, Locke simply assumed the division between property owners and non-property owners as natural, which provided the justification for the wealth of the property owner who invests his labour in his own land. Locke's political arguments were based upon the assumption of a natural right to unequal possessions. It was possible on Locke's argument to obliterate the notion that the ownership of property carried with it a social obligation. In Locke's theory class divisions simply become part of the natural order of society.

These political notions of possessive individualism were also an important part of classical economic thinking, especially in the writings of A. Smith (1723–1790). In his analysis of prices, Smith had argued that the price of any commodity was simply that which was necessary to pay for the grant of the land, the wages of the labourers and the profits of the stock employed in creating and bringing a commodity to the market. A commodity under these conditions sold for its 'natural price' [17]. If the price of a commodity on the market did not conform to these conditions, then Smith expected the forces of economic competition to push the market price towards its natural price. It was economic competition which would bring about a set of circumstances which more contemporary economic theorists called equilibrium. The consequence of Smith's argument is that any government or collective action to change the condition of competition will bring about an artificial economic situation where the natural and the market price of commodities cannot come into equilibrium. To interfere with the competitive character of the market is socially unacceptable in Smith's view, because such intervention would create artificial prices. The organization of social affairs should be guided by the 'invisible hand' of the capitalist market.

Smith's model of the market assumed three significant social classes, namely the owners of capital who acquired profits, the landowners who depended upon rents and the working class which depended upon wages. Following from this class division, Smith was particularly concerned with the explanation of the level of wages in any social formation. He assumed a minimum wage level as that required to replace and maintain the labour force through satisfying needs for food and shelter. He assumed that wages above this minimum would be determined by the relative bargaining capacity of employers and employees, the level of economic activity and the availability of labour.

At times Smith came close to adopting a position developed by T. R. Malthus (1766–1834) who in *Essay on the Principle of Population* had argued that an expansion of the labour force in relation to the available supply of land would bring about starvation and illness unless other steps were taken to control the population supply. Malthus had argued that it was a mistake to increase wages since this would lead to a greater supply of labour which eventually would lead to overcrowding and finally to illness and disease. For Malthus there was a strong demographic pressure on wage levels. Smith at times adopted a similar view in his explanation of inequality of income, but his more general argument was that economic expansion led to increasing wage levels while economic decline led to a reduction in wages. Since Smith assumed that economic decline and stagnation would be more likely than economic growth, he was led to the assumption that wage levels should and would be kept at a minimum. The moral virtue which Smith promoted was thus prudence in a situation of scarcity [18].

There was no space in Smith's economic doctrine for social amelioration of poverty via positive legislation to counteract market forces. Such policies would be important given the natural scarcity of economic situations where low wages would guarantee economic equilibrium and the invisible hand of the market would be to the mutual benefit of all. In this economic theory inequality was not only inevitable but also justifiable.

While many classical and neo-classical economic theories have diverged from Smith's economic analysis, Smithian economics provided the basic conceptual framework for the analysis of market forces and provided the basis for free-market explanations of inequality, especially in the form of income inequality. The attraction of Smith's argument was that it combined the idea of individual rational choice with a view of the unintended consequences of economic action in terms of the invisible hand of the market. That is, individual rationality led to social stability through the unintended consequences of action.

These Smithian assumptions about the invisible hand (that is the reconciliation of egoistic rationalism with social stability) found their way into contemporary economic thought via the work of A. Marshall (1842-1924) in whose work the stability of social and economic relations was always explained on the basis of an assumption about 'the natural order'. Although Marshall was primarily concerned with micro-economic explanations of price levels through demand and supply, he was also concerned with the social consequences of economic life, namely with the causes of poverty. However, his study of economic processes led him to the conclusion that the operation of the market should never be interfered with by the state and he in particular opposed socialist programs of socio-economic reform. Socialist intervention would have disastrous consequences for economic progress by, amongst other things, reducing the level of entrepreneurial activity. Marshall also felt that socialism would seriously interfere with what he called the 'private and domestic relations of life' [19]. Apart from the danger of monopoly in capitalism, Marshall portrayed the economic market system as a benevolent institution of modern society.

One problem with economic analyses of social stability is that they raise questions about the consequences of rational economic behaviour. The classical critique of these assumptions is still to be found in T. Parsons's *The Structure of Social Action* [20]. It was through the theory of action that Parsons provided a critique of individualism and positivism in sociological and economic theory with special reference to the work of Durkheim, Pareto, Weber and Marshall. While much of Parsons's argument is complex and technical, the core of his thesis against positivism is blindingly simple. If one assumes that economic agents behave rationally to achieve their ends, then it is perfectly rational for these economic agents to employ fraud and force. In short there is no good reason for assuming altruistic outcomes from egoistic rationality. Economic behaviour, employing force and fraud, will not lead to a cooperative or stable social system. The stability of the social system has to involve as a minimum a certain degree of consensus about values, ends and procedures. For example, a social system will require agreement about legal norms ruling out theft and fraud as rational and legitimate economic actions. While market stability might be achieved as a consequence of the unintended outcome of individual economic actions, one cannot explain social stability on the basis merely of economic equilibrium. In short, it is necessary to have social and political intervention in the working of the free market in order to achieve a certain level of social stability which would make economic action possible at all. Free markets lead to social anarchy and social anarchy undermines the operation of economic enterprises. To express this differently, the social cost of free market rationality may well outweigh all the gains achieved by entrepreneurship on the basis of egoistic individualism.

Although there has been considerable criticism of both Smithian and Marshallian economic policies, there has been in the modern period a revival of free market economic doctrine by economic theorists like M. Friedman and F. A. Hayek whose theories have been important in the development of recent American and British strategies under the general title of monetarism. Monetarists argue that increasing state intervention in the post-war period brought about a serious decline of profitability, entrepreneurship and economic redevelopment. The level of welfare had reduced the incentive to work and had created unacceptable levels of inflation partly because the money supply had become uncontrollable. Monetarists have sought to denationalize public enterprise, deregulate the market and control the money supply in order to increase profitability.

There is the assumption that in the short run there will be an increase in income inequality and in the distribution of wealth, but in the long run these changes will be acceptable as a consequence of a general increase in the standard of living. The arguments against monetarism in practice are that market forces cannot operate without sufficient state intervention, including state intervention to protect small and new industries against overseas competition. The government is seen not so much as a drain on economic resources but as stimulating economic activity by creating demand through public works. This is one aspect of Keynesian and neo-Keynesian theory which has argued that the instability of the business cycle requires a policy of public works under the control of the state; public expenditure through the multiplier effect stimulates further demand which in turn stimulates a further supply. In periods of economic downturn, Keynesian economic policies create demand in order to create further employment which in turn creates further consumption. Modern monetarism has rejected Keynesian arguments and has suggested that the growth of the state sector is an important feature of modern economic decline in the Western industrial societies where, for example, labour costs have made profits too limited and uncertain for future investment.

These economic arguments have technical difficulties but the underlying set of propositions is relatively straightforward. Economic theory presents us with a choice. The free market in the short run produces massive instability including extreme differentials of income and wealth; but in the long run it produces economic growth which contributes to a general increase in the standard of living. The critics of monetarism argue that the withdrawl of state intervention leads to high rates of liquidation by weak enterprises with a consequent increase in the level of unemployment. The result is a rapid increase in welfare payments for the unemployed which represents a serious tax burden. If the level of payment to the unemployed is reduced, then one consequence is a serious deterioration of social relations exhibited in higher rates of crime especially breaking and entering, suicide and family breakdown. The critics also argue that some social functions and provisions are highly desirable without necessarily being economic in market terms. For example, the provision of parks and play areas for children has a high social value without necessarily being economically viable. Also, while certain aspects of medical care can be provided in a private market (such as cosmetic surgery), some medical functions have to be provided on a public basis (such as services for the aged, the poor and those with chronic illness). Finally, critics of monetarism argue that in the present world economy, local economies which do not receive state protection and encouragement by public policies are overwhelmed by either large multinationals or the economies of stronger nations. In the international market, it is suggested that protectionism is important at least for new and innovative enterprise.

INDIVIDUALISM

In this chapter I have considerd two secular doctrines which have legitimated social inequality, namely Social Darwinism and possessive individualism. These two positions have been important in modern societies with a decline of traditional and religious forms of legitimation. Clearly Darwinism and individualism have much in common since their view of economic markets is parallel. Darwinists saw the economic market as a jungle in which, via struggle, the fittest would survive. Classical economics has seen the market place as an arena of struggle between egoistic rational actors but has argued that the outcome of economic competition is benevolent and progressive. These two forms of legitimation of inequality have in common a strong emphasis on and commitment to the doctrine of individualism. It is commonly suggested in sociology that individualism is indeed the dominant ideology of competitive capitalism and we could thus suggest that Darwinism and utilitarian economics are simply versions of an underlying doctrine, namely the notion of possessive individualism. In this perspective capitalism has little to do with equality but a great deal to do with individualism, competition and inequality.

At a deeper philosophical level, it is also often asserted that there is a necessary contradiction between liberty and equality, where liberty is associated with individualism and equality, with social intervention. Within this dichotomy, any attempt to remove inequality involves considerable state or social intervention to equalize conditions and remove existing privileges but this very intervention must interfere with the individual or private exercise of freedom. The rationalist assumption is that no individual would voluntarily give up his wealth and privilege within an unequal society and as result programs of social equalization must interfere with the democratic rights of the individual. Anti-interventionists tend to argue that only the individual is fully able to know and express his peculiar needs and interests; it is thus inappropriate for the state or some other body to interfere in the life and liberty of the private citizen. Interventionists tend to see this argument as mere ideology, masking an underlying interest in the maintenance of social inequality. Whereas socialists typically regard individualism as a reactionary doctrine, liberals typically regard socialist regulation of the individual as a form of totalitarian politics.

In this chapter I wish to argue that one problem in the traditional discussion of equality versus liberty is that the concept of individualism is frequently too primitive and underdeveloped to be of any significant theoretical value. In order to provide a fuller notion of the individual and individualism, it is useful to distinguish between three forms of individualism. There is firstly the classical doctrine of individualism as it was developed in the seventeenth and eighteenth centuries. Classical individualism was a doctrine which gave special emphasis to the rights and obligations of the individual (especially with respect to property) and this doctrine was oppositional in the sense that it provided a critique of traditional feudalism and hierarchical social relations. As we have seen, Protestantism gave a strong emphasis to the autonomy and separation of the individual, stressing the individual's responsibility to God through a calling in the world. In its economic form, individualism emphasized the importance of achievement and entrepreneurship in the production of wealth, seeing the innovative individual as the catalyst of economic change. Economic individualism gave a significance to private property which had been absent in previous philosophies. Economic individualism was radical insofar as it provided a critique of inherited wealth. For example, Smith was highly critical of the unproductive character of the large landowner who lived off rent without taking any economic risks. In political terms, individualism stresses the political rights of the individual to engage in political action in the pursuit of his own interests, but these political rights were characteristically the exclusive preserve of the property-owner in the liberal philosophy of Locke.

Individualism as the dominant ideology of early capitalism was a belief system which was corrosive of traditional collective modes of existence and practice. In the cultural system of competitive capitalism, the ascetic Protestant was an extension of the isolated Robinson Crusoe of classical economic theory. In summary, individualism may be regarded as a doctrine of individual rights which can be expressed through a variety of dimensions (religious, political, economic and legal). The historical source of this doctrine may be located within Calvinistic Protestantism which revolutionized the traditional notions of conscience and conduct by replacing sacramental institutions with the individual court of conscience [21].

It is possible to distinguish two forms of individualism, namely hedonistic and moral individualism. The doctrine of the autonomy of the individual can be conceptualized in terms of an egoistic and hedonistic individual who rationally calculates social action in order to give him or herself maximum satisfactions regardless of their implications for other individuals. The hedonistic and rational individual is totally asocial, being indifferent to the interests and wishes of others. The hedonistic individual is associated primarily with the early utilitarianism of writers like J. Benthan who attempted to understand the individual in terms of the hedonistic calculus. By contrast, moral individualism stems from the philosophical tradition of I. Kant, E. Durkheim and T. Parsons. In this tradition, the individual is seen as an essentially social being whose personal inclinations and desires can only be fully satisfied in the context of a cooperative social relationship. Durkheim in particular saw the utilitarian and hedonistic form of individualism, stemming from the work of H. Spencer, as destructive of the social order and at least one aspect of the increasing growth of anomic/egoistic suicide in French society in the late nineteenth century. Through his analysis of organic solidarity, Durkheim attempted of develop the notion of moral individualism as a form of belief and practice which would be compatible with the social requirements of modern society; in this moral individualism, the requirements of social solidarity and individual development were perfectly compatible.

This stream of individualism running through Protestantism, political liberalism and classical economics is perfectly compatible with the requirement of equality of opportunity; indeed individualism in this tradition requires as a necessary feature of the social context of the individual an emphasis on the idea of careers open to people with talent. Individualism conceives society as an aggregate of individual agents with very different personal talents and skills. Individualism tends to emphasize the moral benefit of competition and competitive relationships. Consequently competitive individualism requires institutional arrangements of equality of opportunity in order to maximize the effectiveness of differential talent. Radical individualism does not, however, necessarily advocate the importance of equality of condition, since this type of equality tends to ameliorate or minimize the aggressive character of competition. Equality of condition lessens the impact of a competitive race on the individuals involved and therefore what we might call rugged individualism prefers naked competition without social intervention or regulation. In consequence we can say that rationalist individualism is perfectly compatible with equality of opportunity, private property, social inequality and free market capitalism. Indeed as I have suggested earlier, we would expect massive social inequality to be combined with a doctrine of individualism in the context of institutionalized equality of opportunity. This combination of social features with individualism would also require a strong form of impartiality, equity and legality since these conditions would be necessary for the successful emergence of talent and skill through a competitive struggle.

We should distinguish these forms of individualism from the notion of individuality by which I mean a romantic theory of the subjective individual which is focused upon the question of the growth and development of personal sensibility, taste and consciousness. Romantic individuality placed great stress upon inequality, especially inequality between the heroic individual and the mass. Aristocratic individuality emphasized the sheer gap between the mentality of the herd and the exquisite refinement of the wholly individualized person. In the philosophical writing of F. Nietzsche, the authentic personality was a focal point of his view of the importance of transcending conventional moral standards. This view of individuality was critical of bourgeois standards, but it was of course highly elitist. Nietzsche gave special emphasis to the idea of an isolated and alienated intellectual who was separated from the mainstream of bourgeois culture and lived a life subjected to only personal standards. This emphasis in Nietzsche's ethic of the superman eventually found a place in Weber's sociology through the idea of the authority of a charismatic leader. An alternative version of individuality was found in the work of J. S. Mill, S. Kierkegaard and T. Carlyle. In these writers there was the notion that individuality could be developed through education, through spiritual development and through personal moral cultivation. Although these writers retained the notion of undiluted, untrammelled and pristine individuality, they at least allowed for the possibility that any individual could develop individuality through a personal struggle. In short, they did not see the gap between the individual and the mass as an unbridgeable chasm [22].

In modern social thought this emphasis on the uniqueness of the elevated individual has found a philosophical expression in the work of M. Heidegger and the existentialism of J. P. Sartre. In the world of art and drama, the strange and tragic person of A. Artaud probably best encapsulates the whole notion of the existential isolation of the individual from the surrounding culture and society. Artaud's celebration of the irrational in the theatre of cruelty represents a particularly French line of development of the tradition of the isolated genius struggling against the conventional notions of the period. It is important to note that an emphasis of total individuality is also associated with irrationalism and with insanity. The word 'idiot' is derived ultimately from the Greek term of a private person and from the notion of singularity and particularity. The idiot is thus the singular and completely developed person with individuality. These aristocratic notions of individuality would be wholly incompatible with some notion of equality of opportunity, condition or outcome. Aristocratic individuality asserts ontological difference and existential separation. These doctrines tend to be totally opposed to the whole development of welfare and related social regulation.

Finally, there is the distinctive idea of individuation which involves the administrative and bureaucratic separation and identification of persons for the sake of social regulation and social control. In a modern administered society, each citizen will characteristically possess a name, address, insurance number, passport, birth certificate, marriage certificate, driving licence and even an identity card. These tags are administered in order to identify uniquely each person in the interests of social regulation and uniform treatment. Individuation via bureaucracy enforces sameness and equality from a central authority. A number of critical writers on modern society have drawn attention to the function of individuation through the notion of the administered society, through the concept of panopticism and finally through Weber's concept of the iron cage [23]. Whereas individuality emphasizes and insists upon the importance of difference, individuation is an administrative process which aims to establish sameness as the basis of equality. Without bureaucracy and individuation, it would be impossible to provide for equality of condition or bring about equality of outcome.

Individualists therefore commonly associate individuation with egalitarian programs which, in their minds, bring about the disappearance of the individual. In order to institutionalize equality of condition and outcome, it is essential to have a system of bureaucracy, centralized administration and routine instruments for the application of welfare policies. Individuation is essential consequently for bringing about a minimum of social status as a 'necessary ingredient of equal citizenship' [24]. In order for the individual to be developed by education and general social cultivation, it is necessary to provide the individual with a minimum standard of living and health. Citizenship is the institutional framework by which individuals can be developed and cultivated in a modern capitalist environment. Rather than individuation obliterating and limiting the individual, we can see bureaucracy and administration as essential features for regulating the environment in order to permit the individual to become a cultivated and sensitive person. The romantic critique of administration is thus misplaced and clearly elitist. Without a minimum level of welfare, the individual would be the object of illness and social deprivation. Citizenship in these terms makes liberty possible rather than destroying it.

The individualistic critique of equality consequently turns out to be romantic and nostalgic looking back to a society based upon a small community and a stable cultural environment. In the nineteenth century, German social thinking was fundamentally influenced by the work of F. Tönnies (1855–1935) who conceptialized social change in terms of a transition from community (*gemeinschaft*) to society or association (*gesellschaft*) [25]. In a community the individual has a natural, organic and fundamental relationship with the community conceived as a system of reciprocal relationships. Community is a situation based upon trust and intimacy, whereas society is artificial, mechanical and public. Society is a collection of largely anonymous individuals whose separate wills clash in the public arena. In such a society all human beings live for themselves according to egoistic principles. In German social thought this contrast was the basis of a romantic critique of modern society which saw social change as essentially regressive because it destroyed communal links, exposing individuals to the pure forces of the economic market. Public life became conflictual, alienating and anonymous. This nostalgic critique of modernity came to influence Weber's view of the iron cage and G. Simmel's analysis of modern anonymity and estrangement. For Simmel, the development of a money economy brought about an equalization of individuals because exchanges could be precisely measured and quantified, but the result was also that the individual disappeared within the quantitative aggregate of modern industrial society. The development of a money economy brought about a disappearance of the individual under the structure of a regulated economy [26]. The development of a money economy makes possible the development of equality, especially in terms of equity and impartiality, because human behaviour and artefacts can be measured with precise and neutral accuracy. The role of intuition and spontaneous judgement declines.

The romantic critique of money and *gesellschaft* represents a powerful rejection of bureaucracy and standardization. Although the uniformity of economic life may be regarded as a form of alienation, this critique is still nostalgic and romantic because there are positive moral arguments to be made in favour of standardization, where this makes possible a greater degree of impartiality, neutrality and equity. The provision of supplementary benefits or other welfare measures involving money would be impossible in the absence of a money economy and bureaucracy based upon monetary calculations. Whereas Weber often saw bureaucracy in a rather negative fashion, precisely because of its antipathy towards individuality, bureaucracy is actually necessary for the development of equal citizenship and the enjoyment of the benefits brought about by welfare legislation. The alternative to bureaucracy must be either a largely arbitrary system of distribution based upon simply ad hoc decisions or a return to community and *gemeinschaft*; but such a return would appear impossible and utopian given the modern economic, political and demographic structure of modern society. The institutions which characterized community (the village, localism, the church and the family) have been considerably weakened by the advance of modern industrial capitalism and the idea of a return to *gemeinschaft* is quite specifically utopian. In any case, the nostalgic features of Weberian sociology may be suitably abandoned in favour of a more positive evaluation of the merit of monetary calculations, modern systems of administration and the institutions necessary for the full development of citizenship.

IDEOLOGY

In this chapter we have been examining a variety of theodicies (both religious and secular) which simultaneously explain and legitimize various forms of social inequality. We have seen that, in the modern period, inequality has been justified via Darwinism in terms of the survival of the fittest, and through possessive individualism whereby inequality is justified via the apparent naturalness of market processes. However, sociologists often mistakenly write as if the identification of a coherent ideology was the same as explaining its effectiveness. We should not assume that because an ideology is developed by political, economic or religious leaders it is automatically and unambiguously accepted by subordinates. To say, for example, that Darwinism legitimized inequality is not to argue that Darwinism was a dominant ideology, because further evidence would clearly be required concerning the acceptance and implementation of Darwinistic assumptions in everyday practice. We know, for example that Spencer's sociological version of Darwinism was relatively unsuccessful in Britain but enjoyed widespread popularity in the United States of America. Whether or not theodicies receive normative acceptance is in part an empirical question which can be answered by the usual procedures of sociological inquiry. To take one illustration, empirical research suggests that the French working class is far more radical than the British working class. Almost 80 per cent of French workers strongly agreed with the notion that greater effort should be made to reduce income inequality, whereas less than a third of British workers held this opinion [27].

While the question of the effects of ideology may be regarded as a matter of empirical enquiry, I have attempted to argue that there are theoretical reasons for believing in the widespread nature of resistance and opposition to social inequality. While sociologists typically put an emphasis upon the willing acceptance of inequality by subordinate social groups, we should also note that historically the principle of equality (especially as fairness and reciprocity) has been appealed to as the basis for social criticism and change. Peasant revolutions in feudal society often appealed to the notion of equality through the language and mythology of the Bible; for example John Ball, who died in 1381, used as a text for a sermon on the outbreak of the peasant revolt the little poem which goes

When Adam delved and Eve span,
Who was then the gentleman?

During the peasant revolt the notion of an ontological equality was significant in mobilizing peasant opposition to various forms of exploitation from both the clergy and the nobility [28]. Similarly in the English Civil War of the seventeenth century, social criticism was often grounded in a notion of communal equality derived from a conception of the primitive church and in particular the Levellers, as a radical sector of the Puritan Army, were committed to a total redistribution of land and property in England.

In general, we could argue that the concept of justice has been fundamental to a wide range of popular protests against exploitation and has been especially important in millenarian movements which seek a radical and total overthrow of the existing social order through spiritual or supernatural means [29]. Behind these primitive protests against exploitation, there was very often the notion of a social contract which had been broken through colonialism and violence. The idea of a social contract is one of the most basic metaphors of political relations and a contract precisely expresses the notion of balance and reciprocity in social and political affairs. Just as consensus may be justified and explained through the presence of a contract, so also protest and rebellion utilizes the metaphor of contract as the principle whereby opposition is justified. The notion of a social contract is an ancient form of political thought, being closely related to the Jewish idea of a covenant between God and people; the misery of the people is explained through their sinfulness, which represents a departure from this contract. These ideas of fairness, reciprocity and contract give expression to the idea of equity emerging out of the exchange relations which characterize the fabric of all social relationships. The idea of equality is indigenous to social life and this is one explanation of the prominence of the notion of equality in movements of protest, opposition and revolution.

THE SENSE OF INJUSTICE

Sociologists have too readily and too frequently placed an emphasis in their research on the acceptance of inequality by the working class and other subordinate groups. The lower classes and subordinate strata are often presented in Marxist sociology as gullible and incorporated by the capitalist ideology of individualism and consumerism. By contrast, there is ample historical evidence of working-class opposition to exploitation on the grounds of inequality. The selection of examples I have offered is limited but sufficient to indicate the prominence of the idea of justice in social rebellion. Because reciprocity is the basis of social relations, the sense of justice is fundamental to all human interactions. In his justifiably famous discussion of human suffering, B. Moore reflected on the possibility of discovering a universal human feeling and argued that:

there is good evidence for a common substratum of universal human feelings that one can call the sense of injustice. All non-literate people about which I have read are capable of reacting with some sense of outrage when someone both injures them and violates the moral principles of their community. Civilised people, who are often more barbarous than non-literates, can carry this reaction to a point that becomes qualitatively different. Among them too, on the other hand, are obviously similar reactions. Neither ordinary communists nor ordinary westerners like to be victims of police rage, or to hear the tramp of boots on the staircase at night that means prison or concentration camp. [30]

While the dominant class and the political authorities may attempt to render inequality acceptable via the ideology of perfect competition or natural selection or the will of God, there are sociological grounds for arguing that the notion of justice is basic to human life because it is rooted in reciprocity which is the fabric of society itself. If there is a universal emotion it may well be a sense of outrage which emerges from our experience of injustice when the innocent are overwhelmed by superior forces. This notion was the subject of an argument by Berger who also suggested that our sense of injustice and outrage at human suffering was a transcendent experience which could not be relativized [31]. This sense of reciprocity is the fundamental basis of moral action; reciprocity as Durkheim argued is a social fact, that is a moral institution about which we feel strong obligations and which controls or regulates our behaviour. This reciprocity is expressed in such moral propositions as 'do unto others as you would wish them to do unto yourself' and in the maxim of retaliation, namely 'an eye for an eye'. This idea of reciprocity in moral behaviour was the basis therefore of I. Kant's categorical imperative to 'act only on the maxim which you can at the same time will to become a universal law'. These moral norms are not the abstract features of philosophical speculation but the fundamental structures of everyday life. Within a sociological framework, we can argue that everyday life would be impossible without these norms of reciprocity, especially 'keeping a promise, telling the truth, gratitude and elementary loyalty' [32]. When these norms of reciprocity are broken we experience a sense of anger or outrage because the elementary forms of justice have been broken by acts of deviance. While inequality and injustice may be fundamental and inevitable, it also follows as a consquence that our sense of equality and justice is also part of the structure of the social world.

REFERENCES

[1] M. Weber, *The Religion of India: a sociology of Hinduism and Buddhism*, Glencoe Free Press, 1958; B. S. Turner *For Weber, essays of the sociology of fate*, Boston, Routledge & Kegan Paul, 1981, Ch. 4.

[2] M. Weber, *The Sociology of Religion*, London, Methuen, 1968.

[3] P. L. Berger, *The Social Reality of Religion*, London, Faber, 1969; B. S. Turner *Religion and Social Theory, a materialistic perspective*, London, Heinemann, 1983, pp. 80ff.

[4] M. Weber, *The City*, New York, Free Press, 1958, pp. 102–103.

[5] T. Parsons, 'Christianity and modern industrial society' in E. Tiryakian (ed.), *Sociological Theory, Values and Socioculture Change*, New York, Free Press, 1963, pp. 33–70.

[6] M. Weber, *The Protestant Ethic and The Spirit of Capitalism*, London, Allen & Unwin, 1930.

[7] A. O. Lovejoy, *The Great Chain of Being: a study of the history of an idea*, Cambridge, Cambridge University Press, 1938.

[8] D. Pipes, *Slave Soldiers and Islam, the genesis of a military system*, New Haven and London, Yale University Press, 1981.

[9] C. R. Boxer, *The Dutch Seaborne Empire*, London, Hutchinson, 1965.

[10] G. L. Smith, *Religion and Trade in New Netherland, Dutch origins and American development*, Ithaca and London, Cornell University Press, 1973.

[11] J. Rex, *Race Relations in Sociological Theory*, London, Weidenfeld & Nicolson, 1970.

[12] J. Howard, *Darwin*, Oxford, Oxford University Press, 1982; J. D. Y. Peel, *Herbert Spencer, the evolution of a sociologist*, London, Heinemann, 1971.

[13] J. W. Burrow, *Evolution and Society, a study in Victorian social theory*, Cambridge, Cambridge University Press, 1966; R. Bierstedt, *Power and Progress, essays on sociological theory*, New York, McGraw-Hill, 1974, Ch. 6.

[14] R. Hofstadter, *Social Darwinism in American Thought*, Boston, Beacon Press, 1944.

[15] M. Sahlins, *The Use and Abuse of Biology, an anthropological critique of sociobiology*, London, Tavistock, 1977.

[16] C. B. Macpherson, *The Political Theory of Individualism, Hobbes to Locke*, Oxford, Clarendon Press, 1962, p. 54; E. K. Hunt *Property and Prophets, the evolution of economic institutions and ideologies*, New York, Harper & Row, 1981.

[17] A. Smith, *The Wealth of Nations*, London, Methuen, 1961, Vol. 1, p. 62.

[18] S. S. Wolin, *Politics and Vision*, London, Allen & Unwin, 1961, p. 330.

[19] A. Marshall, *Principles of Economics*, London, Macmillan, 1961, p. 713.

[20] T. Parsons, *The Structure of Social Action*, New York, McGraw-Hill, 1937.

[21] B. Nelson, 'Conscience and the making of early modern cultures: the Protestant Ethic beyond Max Weber', *Social Research*, **36**(4), pp. 4–21; M. Hepworth and B. S. Turner, *Confession, studies in deviance and religion*, London, Routledge & Kegan Paul, 1982.

[22] A. L. Le Quesne, *Carlyle*, Oxford, Oxford University Press, 1982.

[23] M. Jay, *Adorno*, London, Fontana, 1983, p. 22; M. Foucault, *Discipline and Punish, the birth of the prison*, Harmondsworth, Peregrine, 1979.

[24] R. Dahrendorf, 'Liberty and equality' in *Essays in the Theory of Society*, London, Routledge & Kegan Paul, 1968, p. 197.

[25] F. Tönnies, *Community and Association*, Michigan, Michigan State University Press, 1957.

[26] G. Simmel, *The Philosophy of Money*, Boston and London, Routledge & Kegan Paul, 1978.

[27] D. Gallie, *Social Inequality and Class Radicalism in France and Britain*, Cambridge, Cambridge University Press, 1983, p. 70; S. Lash, *The Militant Worker, class and radicalism in France and America*, London, Heinemann, 1984; C. Tilly, L. Tilly and R. Tilly, *The Rebellious Century 1830–1968*, Cambridge, Mass., Harvard University Press, 1975; E. Shorter and C. Tilly, *Strikes in France 1830–1968*, Cambridge, Mass., Harvard University Press, 1974.

[28] F. Engels, *The Peasant War in Germany*, Moscow, Progress Publishers, 1974

[29] E. J. Hobsbawm, *Primitive Rebels*, Manchester, Manchester University Press, 1959.

[30] Barrington Moore, Jr., *Reflections on the Causes of Human Misery and upon Certain Proposals to Eliminate Them*, London, Allen Lane, 1970, p. 52.

[31] P. L. Berger, *A Rumor of Angels*, New York, Doubleday, 1969.

[32] A. Heller, *Everyday Life*, London, Routledge & Kegan Paul, 1984, p. 85.

5

Experiments in Equality

UTOPIAN SOCIAL MOVEMENTS

Although human societies are invariably unequal, throughout human history there have been innumerable attempts to reduce or eradicate human inequality by a series of experiments in equality. Social movements and social groups have been organized as alternative systems which have sought radical means to reduce or expunge the inequalities of power, wealth and prestige that are characteristic of conventional society. In pre-modern times, millenarian movements have challenged the existing social structure in the name of a utopian system which would replace the existing forms of inequality. In medieval times a great variety of these millenarian groups drew inspiration from the Christian conception of the primitive church in which it was assumed there had been a fundamental equality between believers. Before the Reformation, Christian teaching about the millennium had a strong attraction to the lower social strata, especially among the uprooted and dispossessed peasantry who were being dragged into urban society as beggars. Fantasies about a future kingdom of equality provided an ideology which mobilized these groups to transfrom their social circumstances [1].

It can be argued that pre-modern societies were dominated by two contrasted forms of belief, one which suggested that the present order was essentially unstable, and a contrary set of dominant beliefs which asserted the stability of existing circumstances. K. Mannheim noted the important role of utopian beliefs in mobilizing the poor to reject the existing social structure and culture in the name of an egalitarian society which would be constructed out of the destruction of the existing order [2]. These millenarian movements continued to be important in depressed urban society among the poor where utopian opposition to exploitation often became transformed into political conflict of a more secular variety [3]. In primitive societies which have been undermined by the impact of colonial domination and neo-colonial economic exploitation, these millenarian movements have often assumed the form of cargo cults which have organized tribal groups into movements of social protest aimed at removing white domination. These cults have also asserted the importance of equality through a redistribution of the expected cargo to all members of the movement [4].

The anthropological analysis of millenarian movements has suggested that active millenarianism typically leads towards secular politics and trade union organization. Cargo cults provide the prototype for political organization in traditional societies. Where the cargo cult is destroyed by political opposition from the white community, millenarianism typically becomes passive, quiescent and individualistic. The implication of this research is that utopian social movements have a limited life span before they are either undermined or transformed into alternative social movements. The same implication also exists with respect to religious sects, communes and alternative communities.

In the history of Christianity, the sect as a social type has been of major significance in the development of religious organization and consciousness [5]. The sect typically breaks away from the church in order to reject formalism, hierarchy, priestly authority and the departure from the ideals of the early church. These religious sects commonly adopted an egalitarian ideal with respect to the redistribution of property and the reduction of hierarchies of power; they also occasionally adopted a communal organization of sexuality as an expression of a radical egalitarianism. In the seventeenth century during the period of the English Civil War, a number of radical religious sects (such as the Levellers and Fifth Monarchy Men) emerged in protest against the existing distribution of wealth in a society dominated by the land-owning aristocracy and the gentry. In more recent history a great variety of utopian sects and alternative communes developed in nineteenth-century America among the lower strata of European settlers. These utopian communities sought a perfect society in the new world of North America where there was space and opportunity to develop small-scale alternative commmunities. The Rappites and Amana Society founded separate communities as the best means of creating an egalitarian and sectarian society where individuals could seek their own salvation. Other groups such as the Hutterians and Amish communities sought, by means of physical and social exclusion, to preserve and establish the immutability of traditional lifestyle and custom.

One of the most interesting and important of these utopian sects was the Oneida Community of perfectionists who established themselves in New York State [6]. The Oneida community developed under the leadership of a Congregationalist minister called John Humphrey Noyes who held to the idea that human beings could attain total perfection through the development of an egalitarian community where they would become secure from sin. In this society complete communism was to be developed as the basis for a holy existence and this communism was to create egalitarianism not only in the distribution of property but also in sexual relationships. The Oneida perfectionalism developed a variety of institutions for controlling deviance within the community such as the practice of self-criticism and mutual exhortation. The Oneida community flourished for some forty years before internal tensions and external opposition forced the community to abandon much of its original communism.

Within the sociology of religion it is commonly argued that sectarian social groups have a very limited lifespan, often for only one generation. The paradox is that where sects are successful, they necessarily grow in size and scale, and this development brings about the requirement for a system of authority, property relations, internal discipline and the development of formal social institutions. The sect is transformed from an oppositional group into a conformist denomination through the development of its own industry, teaching, Sunday school system and other denominational structures. This process of denominationalization is particularly prevalent amongst so-called conversionist sects which are committed to widespread evangelization of society [7]. These studies of religious groups suggest that the reduction or elimination of inequality may be achieved within a small-scale institution, isolated from the wider social structure; but this reduction of inequality may be historically limited. Alternative religious communities tend over time to develop a hierarchy of authority, a formal organization of sexual relationships, a system for the control of property and forms of bureaucratic arrangements for the regular accomplishment of social tasks. In Britain for example, there was an important upsurge in alternative religious communities as part of a wider development of communes, but many of these failed to survive for more than a few years [8]. Few of these alternative communes solved the problem of authority and the institutional organization of decision making without undermining their own egalitarian doctrines.

The search for egalitarian social organizations is not of course confined to religious movements but has formed part of the secular socialist tradition of the nineteenth and twentieth centuries. For example, in Britain social experiments were conducted to change the nature of production and ownership in order to achieve an egalitarian redistribution of wealth with a reduction in the social division of labour. R. Owen (1771–1858) created a model village for workers in New Lanark where he attempted to combine private property in the means of production with socialized distribution. The model village incorporated communal facilities, social welfare and a system of education for all. A similar development took place under the inspiration of W. Morris (1834–1896) who sought to restore the dignity of labour and the wholeness of life through the assertion of craft industry. The development of a new system of craft production would require a major social transformation and he argued for a policy of socialist reform which included the development of common ownership and the establishment of workers' cooperatives dedicated to manufacture in the spirit of traditional craftsmanship. Morris's ideal of craft was based upon a conception of production which had existed in medieval times and this utopian vision of craftsmanship was a combination of socialism and cultural conservatism which had an important impact on British art and design.

THE KIBBUTZ EXPERIMENT

A far more radical form of egalitarian experiment developed through the influence of Zionism which was a political movement seeking to resettle Jewish communities in Palestine in order to transform the traditional Jewish lifestyle of the European ghettos. Zionism began in Basle in 1897 when T. Herzel organized the first world Zionist conference with the aim of promoting the aspirations of Jews to return to the land of Israel where they would establish a Jewish state. The Zionist movement came eventually to argue that the Jewish communities in Israel should be established without the help of Arab labour and these communities should develop a new egalitarian socialist system which found its highest expression in the ideals of the kibbutz. The kibbutz is a cooperative agricultural settlement which is owned by its members and in which the family unit is replaced by a system of common care and protection for children. This commune was organised in opposition to private property and attempted to minimize the social division of labour in order to undermine the traditional separation of mental and manual labour. A number of experiments were attempted to train children collectively in the spirit of common activity and collective endeavour. The kibbutz experiment was first introduced in Israel in 1909 to create a system of Jewish settlement which would function within a market economy while being socially independent.

The kibbutz system was originally welcomed by a number of socialist commentators as an important experiment in communitarian development which could be imitated in other developing societies [9]. However, the kibbutz system has also been subject to considerable criticism which rejects the idea that this experiment was genuinely socialist. It is argued that the kibbutz was in fact an institution for the military domination of Palestine at the expense of the original Arabic inhabitants. The kibbutz was a system of colonization which in fact depended upon Arab labour and exploited the indigenous Palestinian population [10]. It is also claimed that over time the collective family structure of the kibbutz declined and was replaced by the typical nuclear family structure of more conventional societies [11]. The main point of this criticism is that egalitarian experiments have to be seen in a broader social context. The kibbutz was an institution where the division of labour could be reduced because the kibbutz was dependent upon the wider social organization of Israel for the provision of essential services. The members of the kibbutz represent approximately 3 per cent of the Israeli population and their socialist experiment is parasitic upon the continuity of inequality in the larger social context [12].

PEASANT REVOLUTIONS

Sectarian and millenarian movements appear to arise primarily in periods of rapid social change when traditional patterns of life are disrupted, often as a consequence of the incorporation of a village or tribe within the world market system of capitalism. These protest movements which frequently asserted the importance of equality were responses to these patterns of global disruption and they were conservative social movements since they looked backwards to the re-establishment of traditional patterns of life. In the contemporary period the struggle for social equality has often been associated with the emergence of a traditional peasantry as a political factor in modern revolutions [13].

We can identify broadly three conditions which give rise to peasant revolutions. The first is a demographic crisis where a sudden increase in the peasant population, as a consequence of changes in food production and social medicine, transforms the ratio of population to land, bringing about a serious economic crisis. Secondly, there is an ecological crisis which arises with the alienation of the peasantry from the land, the undermining of traditional forms of subsistence farming and the increasing dominance of the market in association with the development of cash-crops for export. Finally, there is a crisis of authority since the traditional leaders of the peasant society are replaced by entrepreneurs and officials who are not part of the traditional social structure of the peasant village. The peasant becomes subject to new patterns of exploitation by outsiders who do not understand or share the assumptions of peasant society [14]. Within the moral outlook of the traditional peasantry, the experience of reciprocity and subsistence was fundamental to the idea of justice as equal exchange. When peasant societies are sucked into the global system of the capitalist market, their traditional notions of reciprocity and fairness are undermined and their sense of relative deprivation contributes to the increasingly radical character of peasant consciousness and protest movements [15].

While Marx had argued that the peasantry was not important in the formation of modern revolutionary movements, the experience of revolution in Algeria, Cuba, Mexico and China has depended significantly on the evolution of peasant radicalness and involvement in the revolutionary process.

Peasant values and institutions came to play a major part in the development of communism in China under the leadership of Mao Tse-tung. We can only understand Mao's peasant revolution if we grasp the character of China in the 1920s which was still economically an under-developed society. As a consequence there was virtually no urban proletariat within the social structure of China and the Communist Party had therefore to depend significantly on the peasantry as the largest social class in the prerevolutionary period. Mao insisted on the centrality of the countryside in the transformation of China and on the active part which the peasantry would have to play in the creation of a socialist China.

Throughout the nineteenth century, there had been a major economic decline in China leading to the undermining of the peasant position in society, the abandonment of villages and the deterioration of the irrigation system. This was also a period of significant peasant protest and violence resulting in either large-scale peasant uprisings or banditry. The peasantry was increasingly in debt and exploitation of the peasant by the landlord and the merchant had grown significantly. The Chinese Communist Party in the twentieth century was able to draw upon and organize this indigenous tradition of peasant protest. The turning point in the development of Chinese communism was the Japanese occupation which had the un-intended consequence of solidifying and organizing Chinese opposition. The initial aim of the revolution was to redistribute land away from the wealthy to the poor peasant in order to unite the peasant and the agricultural labourer against the rich peasants and the traditional landlord. However, because the land was redistributed to individuals on an equal share basis, the Communist Party broke the family basis of the village and by undermining kinship formed a direct link between the peasant commune and the national government [16].

Although there is major disagreement as to the character of Maoism, a number of writers have argued that Chinese communism represents a radical peasant utopia in which the language of Western Marxism was imposed upon a movement which had its real origins in the Chinese countryside. The genius of Mao lay in the fusion of Marxist/Leninism with the practice of rural revolution and the adaptation of western political philosophy to the needs of a peasant guerrilla movement. As Mao argued, in China the revolutionary movement came from the country to the town rather than vice versa and consequently Mao, against both Marx and Lenin, stressed the importance of the peasant as a revolutionary agent [17].

In Maoism there was an important emphasis on the idea of the community and the goal of revolution was the establishment of a special form of communal relationships based upon cooperative ideals without the specialization associated with an advanced social division of labour and without the distinctions characteristic of status and class. Manual labour was regarded as morally superior to mental activity and intellectual labour had to be incorporated in manual labour. The existence of a basic peasant society and culture had to be taken as the fundamental premise of economic development. Large holdings of land were broken up for poor peasants and some forms of private industry were tolerated within very strict limits. However, in 1952 there was the development of centralized planning for industry and agirculture and in 1955 agriculture was collectivized by means of cooperatives and eventually by public ownership, although peasants were allowed to maintain small private plots of land for production.

The attempt to industrialize China was initially a failure and in 1958 under Mao's leadership the Party announced the program of a 'great leap forward' which was to bring about a massive increase in productivity with an economic rate of growth amounting to 25 per cent. By 1961 it was clear that the 'great leap forward' had been an economic catastrophe and the standard of living of the peasantry had declined significantly. Mao then turned to a different political strategy which became the Cultural Revolution of the 1960s and this program was designed to transform the attitude and mentality of the masses. The result was massive conflict between those Party members who were loyal to the bureaucracy and the Red Guards who attempted to organize the youth of the big cities in support of Mao and the Cultural Revolution.

For Mao the Cultural Revolution was merely an illustration of the theory of permanent revolution since Maoism argued that the political stabilization of a society always led inevitably to the development of privilege and the emergence of a new bureaucratic class. In order to prevent the emergence of social stratification in terms of privilege and prestige, it was necessary for the revolutionary masses periodically to destroy the bureaucracy and other forms of hierarchical distinction based upon the universities and elite institutions. The antagonism towards the universities and formal education reflected the centrality of the peasantry to Maoism and the prestige given to physical labour. Maoism emphasized the importance of character education through hard work and manual employment as a central aspect of the egalitarian ideal of Chinese communism. As a populist leader of the peasantry, Mao explicitly argued that education through the study of books could be harmful to the moral character of the individual and that the university-trained intellectual needed periodically to be retrained through employment in the villages. Behind this ideal of radical egalitarianism which would destroy the division between mind and hand in a permanent revolution, there was also the presence of a traditional peasant hatred of elite culture and the values of the educated city dweller.

Critics of Maoism argue that while there was the development of peasant egalitarianism, there was relatively little political equality in China where planning and decision making were controlled by a small elite which was jealous to preserve its monopoly over political information. Equality of condition has obliterated other forms of equality and the Chinese population is regulated by an administrative structure which leaves little room for initiative or individual choice. The development of a fertility program limiting women to one successful pregnancy per lifetime represents a form a Malthusian regulation which would be difficult without the domination of the Party over everyday life. The importance of centralization and cultural uniformity has also had very negative consequences for religious and ethnic minorities in contemporary China [18]. However, those commentators who were sympathetic to the Chinese experiment drew attention to the important efforts made to secure social equality by not using wage differentials as economic incentives and not permitting the emergence of elite groups of managers or technicians. Despite poor harvests and delayed economic growth, the Chinese communists have succeeded in ending famine and plague in a society which faces massive population and production problems [19].

It is difficult unfortunately to locate precise statistical measurements of China's successes and failures since social investigation had been discouraged during Mao's cultural domination of China [20]. The limited evidence which we do possess suggests that social stratification in China has not been eliminated despite the draconian measures of the Cultural Revolution [21]. Furthermore, China has over the last twenty years made fundamental changes to its foreign policy showing a greater willingness to form alliances with Western powers against both Vietnam and Russia [22]. More importantly, in the 1980s the Chinese leadership adopted radically different economic and political strategies which were in part modelled on Western, free-market capitalism. There is now a greater emphasis on wage differentials, individualism, enterprise and initiative. China has also shown interest in recruiting Western intellectuals to transform the curriculum of Chinese universities and there has been a superficial adoption of Western dress and styles of living. If this process of encouraging the market to develop in China were to continue, then we would expect increasing wage differentials and ultimately an increase in prestige differences and other forms of cultural inequality. Given the volatile character of recent Chinese politics,it is not clear whether this line of development could be pursued indefinitely without considerable resistance from those Party leaders and intellectuals who still adhere to a Maoist philosophy of the revolution.

STRATIFICATION IN STATE SOCIALISM

Whereas it is difficult to document precisely levels of income, wealth and prestige in China, the evidence bearing upon social stratification within the Soviet bloc, and specifically for Russia itself, is far more ample and well-developed. After the revolution of 1917 the USSR emerged from the First and Second World Wars with severe devastation of its population and resources. Under J. Stalin (1879–1953) Russia went through a period of collectivization and industrialization from above. Becoming the supreme leader of the Soviety Party and State in 1929, Stalin organized a process of extreme political centralization which provided the basis for the suppression of dissent and the control of the whole society in the interests of rapid industrialization. Under Stalinism there eventually emerged a Soviet power elite which enjoyed considerable privileges under the new system of totalitarian power, but there is evidence that there was a process of egalitarian redistribution taking place in both the USSR and its satellite societies.

It has been argued by F. Parkin that we can distinguish two phases of socialist development: in the first stage of socialist reconstruction, there is a significant redistribution of wealth and power, but in the later phases of industrialization the old system of class and prestige inequality re-emerges with the development of a free market [23]. With the growing dominance of the Party and the redistribution of control of the means of production, there was a significant improvement in the standards of living of the underprivilged and disprivileged throughout East Europe with the introduction of welfare, social security and tax reform. The wage differential between various workers (manual, white collar and professional) was significantly reduced from their pre-war position. In Czechoslovakia for example, clerical workers earned on average 20 per cent less than manual workers in the post-war period. Similar developments took place in Poland and Yugoslavia. As a consequence of a system of positive discrimination to change the character of equality of condition in favour of the working class, there were significant improvements in the recruitment of working people to the educational system. In 1949, 66 per cent of the university population of Hungary were from the working and peasant classes compared with 11 per cent in the pre-socialist era. In Yugoslavia by 1951, 35 per cent of the university population were from manual working-class background, while in Poland by 1961 more than 48 per cent of university and college students were from peasant and working class backgrounds. In East Europe generally, there were important changes in the prestige ranking of occupations so that occupations associated with private property and commerce declined in social estimation whereas there was a significant improvement in the social status of skilled workers and intellectuals. These improvements in the rewards distributed to lower classes arose from the political need of the new ruling group to consolidate its position in society and to reward its followers. However with growth of industrialism in Eastern Europe, there developed a growing tension between the system of rewards which is required by socialist ideology and the technical needs of industrial efficiency and market rationality. The consequence of industrialism was to increase the wages of engineers and technicians. The income distribution of these societies became more inegalitarian and there was also an increase in the levels of unemployment throughout Eastern Europe. The proportion of Communist Party members drawn from the manual class declined in the 1950s and 1960s while there was a corresponding increase in the representation of skilled and professional workers.

The crucial difference between capitalist and socialist society is the relative importance of politics and economics in the distribution of rewards. In capitalism it is primarily the market mechanism which accounts for the inequality of income, prestige and employment, whereas in socialist society it is the political dimension which explains social differences. In state socialism, loyalty to the Party is the primary criterion for the enjoyment of major social benefits. In short, it is the power nexus rather than the cash nexus which explains the character of social stratification in the USSR and the Soviet satellite societies. The nature and level of social inequality in the Soviet Union are known with some degree of precision. In the Soviet Union there is an unsatisfactory provision of luxury and other consumer goods, but there are also shortages of basic supplies such as milk, vegetables and household goods. In this situation a high-ranking official with a reasonable salary may in fact have some difficulty in spending his income. In these circumstances there has evolved a system of distribution via rations which provides a reward system for Party members and high-ranking officials. This system is called the 'kremlin ration' and the 'academic ration' but there are other forms of redistribution which are centred on the existence of a closed shop or distributor in the main cities [24]. Russia has also experienced a severe crisis of housing, both in quantity and quality. The provision of better housing for the party elite is consequently an important feature of the prestige system of the society. In addition to housing, there are restrictions on the production of motor cars and the ownership or use of such vehicles has a significant place in the distribution of prestige. Other features of the inequality of distribution would include education, special medical services, holiday facilities and foreign travel.

The inequalities in income, prestige and other rewards are associated with political access to the redistributive system where some combination of Party membership and educational achievement is crucial in the explanation of these inequalities. There are other dimensions of inequality in the Soviet Union which would include rural/urban differences, differences between the sexes, and forms of social inequality related to ethnic and cultural background. Inequality as a consequence of religious or national identity is especially prevalent in the Soviet Union [25]. In summary, the principal social cleavages of these state-socialist societies are firstly the division between the urban working class and the peasantry, then the cleavage between the manual and non-manual labouring classes and finally the division between the Party and the professional strata whose privileges flow from their technical and administrative knowledge [26].

There are clearly important differences between these societies. Some writers have argued that China is a more open and democratic socialist experiment permitting considerable public debate [27]. There have also been interesting experiments in workers' control over industrial production in a number of East European societies which have been taken by Western observers as significant models of industrial democracy [28]. As a generalization, however, there is relatively little disagreement that state-socialist societies are stratified in terms of privilege, power and prestige. Although social classes in terms of the ownership of private property may have disappeared, there has been an important continuity of other forms of inequality and stratification. There are a variety of explanations for this continuity of social stratification in societies which have adopted a variety of socialist measures to eradicate inequality.

It can be suggested that the significant feature of Russian society is its historical continuity and the present system of political control from a centralized Party represents a continuing history of despotism. For example, K. Wittfogel identified a special type of society which he called the 'hydraulic social system' in which the state became the dominant social institution because the state was required to regulate the production system based upon irrigation [29]. The state emerged as the centralized owner of property and the guardian of legitimacy and power within a society where the bureaucracy and the official social strata were the controlling agents of state power. Within these hydraulic societies there developed a political system of total power because the whole apparatus of control was focused on the state. Wittfogel's notion of 'oriental despotism' was simply a twentieth-century version of Marx's concept of the Asiatic mode of production. Marx and Engels had referred to Tsarist Russia as 'semi-Asiatic' in 1853. Engels claimed that the isolation of the commune in peasant Russian society was the institutional basis of oriental despotism in his book *Anti-Dühring* in 1877. After Marx and Engels, there were prolonged debates in Russian Marxism as to the character of traditional Russian society. Some critics regarded the peasant commune as the origin of Russian absolutism whereas other writers saw the commune as the basis for socialist development. The crux of the problem was that Stalinism looked like a communist version of traditional Russian despotism where the state was dominant and the institutions of civil society were underdeveloped. The inequalities of modern Russia are seen in this perspective to be features of political despotism so that the revolution merely reinstated the traditional sources of power.

There is also a tradition which stems from L. Trotsky (1879–1940) and which gives particular prominence to the dominant social role of the bureaucracy as that class which has replaced the capitalists as the main exploiters of the population in state socialism. Socialist democracy has been undermined by the dead hand of bureaucratic management, regulation and control. This bureaucratic class model of state socialism has received its most prominent explanation through the work of R. Bahro, M. Djilas and M. Schachtman [30]. Other theorists have detected a convergence between socialist and capitalist societies towards the managerial state in which the main economic institutions are controlled and managed by a new class. The state in both capitalism and socialism becomes more interventionist and the traditional ruling class of property owners is replaced by a new class of managers who seek social and global dominance through the new bureaucracies. These managers will ultimately exercise their political control over the means of production and gain privilege in the distribution of products. In a sense the state becomes their property. Within the Soviet Union this managerial class will seek to reduce the capitalist world to political and economic impotence, to regulate the masses in a way which will make then compliant to managerial ideology and legitimacy, and finally to compete amongst themselves for the management of the privilege system based upon rations and scarcity [31]. For other commentators, it is not the coherence of the bureaucratic class which explains the continuity of elite power but rather the fragmentation of the masses which provides the basis for totalitarianism [32].

These different explanations of inequality in state socialism give prominence to the political determination of inequality and by implication give prominence to the economic market in generating inequality in capitalism. We need therefore to return to the question of the complicated relationship between political and economic processes in the determination of social inequality under different social systems. The unregulated activity of the market in Western capitalist societies appears to be closely related to the development of inequality, especially in terms of income. Of course to this explanation we need to add the role of the traditional family in the inheritance of wealth and the role of educational institutions in reinforcing the impact of family-centred cultural capital. It has been assumed (by writers like F. Parkin) that in socialist societies the reintroduction of the market place necessarily leads to greater inequality.

This perspective has been challenged by writers like I. Szelenyi on the grounds that we cannot assume that the market will operate in exactly the same way under entirely different social conditions; that is, we cannot assume that market inequality in a capitalist context will have the same social and economic function in a socialist context. Through his study of the housing market in Hungary, Szelenyi came to the conclusion that paradoxically a free market for the production and distribution of housing would increase equality in Hungary rather than lead to an intensification of housing inequality. Whereas in capitalist society the labour market is a central institution, the core institution of state-socialist redistribution systems is the non-market trade of labour. The welfare state in capitalism tends to redistribute income where this income is first defined in the labour market, but under state socialism the state redistributes the economic surplus which was directly realized in the central state budget. In socialism (as institutionalized in the Soviet bloc) the primary social antagonism is between the immediate producers and those classes which redistribute wealth through the state apparatus [33]. In capitalism the political process within the democratic system creates the possibilities for citizenship rights, but the economy generates major inequalities of wealth and income.

If we accept Szelenyi's argument, then in state-socialist societies it is the political arena under the dominance of a bureaucratic class acting on behalf of the state which is the arena of social inequality, and the expansion of a free market sector within the economy would probably generate a greater degree of equality and personal freedom. It is certainly the case that the working classes of East European societies have relatively little political or economic freedom, since the tradition of citizenship rights is regarded as bourgeois and there is little scope in the economy for personal autonomy. The Soviet satellite societies have been recently criticized in these terms since

the working majority of the population in East European societies has no control over the conditions, process or results of its own labour. Not only the technical organisation or the process of production, but also all the social-economic decisions concerning what to produce and to employ the gross product socially are actually established and made by a distinct and separate social group (the bureaucracy) whose corpus is continuously replenished through the mechanisms of a selective cooptation and which is essentially self-appointed (its rule being in fact based, to use Trotsky's famous formulation, on a right of primogeniture of power). The dependence of direct producers on this dominant group is so extensive that they have no effective and direct power of bargaining, either individually or collectively, over their own share in the gross national product. [34]

By contrast it is the relative autonomy of the political from the economic in capitalist societies which creates the opportunity for the development of citizenship rights of welfare equality as an outcome of popular struggle, trade union organization and working-class resistance to the unregulated effects of the market place.

DISCUSSION

In this chapter I have examined a variety of experiments in equality. There are millenarian and religious movements which seek to establish an equal society through the intervention of supernatural powers brought about by the use of ritual, prayer and magic. There are also utopian communities which, in North America, sought to achieve an ideal society and a communal form of existence, often by geographical and social isolation form the wider society. These utopian sects partly achieved equality through the reduction of the social division of labour, the redistribution of wealth and the regulation of the family and sexual life through communal means. Socialist experiments in equality attempted, through such schemes as Owen's model village, to bring about market socialism whereby production would take place in a non-competitive environment. In the twentieth century many youth movements have attempted to achieve a naive simplicity of life through the development of small communes which would practise a communal ideal in terms of sexual and social equality at the interpersonal level. By contrast, there have been far more radical processes of secular and socialist equality through the Zionist kibbutz which regulated the family, undermined the division between mental and manual labour, set up cooperative agricultural production and sought to realize a Jewish territorial solution to the traditional insecurity of the ghetto. These social movements were relatively small-scale, involving limited groups of people in direct socialist experiments. By contrast, the attempt to create macro-equality by revolutionary means in China and Russia involved millions of people in a social reconstruction of backward societies. We have seen that that Chinese communist experiment involved the assertion of peasant values and institutions as the means for social development and economic growth on a communal basis. The Russian communist revolution involved a centralized attempt to bring about rapid industrial development through collectivization and forced movements of population; it also involved a severe restriction on the production of consumption goods in favour of investment in heavy industry.

By way of generalization, the sociological evidence relating to these societies and social groups suggests that these experiments in equality were historically unsuccessful and that inequality came to characterize these special groups and movements regardless of their size, ideology, goals and social contexts. Sects tend to become denominations over time where the traditional authority of the minister of religion is reasserted; utopian communes tend to collapse once their charismatic founders have died or they continue under the official control of some committee or authoritarian leadership. The kibbutz have been criticized as merely military outposts for the colonial intentions of Israeli society. The Chinese revolution has not brought about a permanent redistribution of wealth and traditional inequalities between occupational groups appear to be re-emerging. Finally, while in Russia differences of social wealth based upon economic ownership have largely disappeared, there is massive inequality in terms of income, prestige and rewards which appear to be based upon bureaucratic power.

Social inequality appears to be continuous or difficult to obliterate for reasons which were central to Weber's sociology of power. All social groups are forced to make decisions about the allocation of resources, the treatment of deviance, the protection of the group and the selection of long-term social objectives. Although these decisions can be based upon an on-going democratic and equal discussion, some form of central decision-making appears to develop because it is often difficult to resolve disputes and disagreements by a democratic consensus. There is the necessity to impose decisions where there are genuine disagreements within social groups. Furthermore some sections of the community may be more expert either because of education or experience, and expert knowledge acquires a certain privileged status. In order for the group to function at all, there must be a system of authority, whether or not this is regarded as legitimate. The achievement of permanent and absolute equality is consequently very problematic, since there will be an incipient growth of inequality around the question of authority and power in all human relationships. In addition to this problem of power and authority, there are more obvious problems such as the regulation of sexuality, the reproduction of children, the education of these offspring and the control over the family and household. Despite criticism of the Davis and Moore theory of social stratification, there appears to be a permanent problem of motivation in human societies whereby it is necessary to induce individuals to fulfil social roles which may be dangerous, demanding or onerous. The problem of motivation does not appear to be simply the artefact of a bourgeois competitive society. There are other problems of equality relating to the inevitable aging of human beings, their retirement from direct labour and their increasing subjection to illness and disease. The aged, even under the most favourable social circumstances, often become the objects of stigma and victimization (however, mild or indirect this may appear).

The sociology of equality tends therefore to be a pessimistic inquiry into the inevitability of inequality. Many sociologists would come ultimately to the conclusion suggested by Weber, namely that the inequality of power is not only inevitable but necessary to the very functioning of society. In this book, however, I have suggested a slightly different set of conclusions, namely that although inequality constantly re-emerges in human societies we appear to have a 'natural' sense of fairness and justice which develops out of the reciprocity that determines the contours of everyday life. Opposition, conflict and resistance to inequality seems as inevitable as in equality itself. Therefore as sociologists we should expect the constant re-emergence of social movements, groups and revolutions which seek to bring about an egalitarian redistribution of social wealth, prestige and power. Although we might expect these revolutions to 'fail' over a long period of time this would not be an argument against social change or redistribution. The sociological evidence simply suggests that utopian notions of absolute justice and equality should be regarded as utopian, but some practical measures towards greater equality are always open to us and morally always desirable. Religious sects, utopian communes, workers cooperatives and massive social revolutions did achieve significant advances in equality between men and women, between social classes, between national groups and between rural and urban communities. Although over many generations they experience the redevelopment and reassertion of political and social inequality, we should not deny their achievement any more than we should be blind to their failures.

REFERENCES

[1] N. Cohn, *The Pursuit of the Millenium*, London, Secker & Warburg, 1957.

[2] K. Mannheim, *Ideology and Utopia*, London, Routledge & Kegan Paul, 1936.

[3] E. J. Hobsbawm, *Primitive Rebels, studies in archaic forms of social movements in the 19th and 20th centuries*, Manchester, Manchester University Press, 1959.

[4] P. Worsley, *The Trumpet shall Sound*, London, MacGibbon & Kee, 1957.

[5] E. Troeltsch, *The Social Teaching of the Christian Churches*, New York, Macmillan, 1931.

[6] B. Wilson, *Religious Sects*, London, Weidenfeld & Nicolson, 1970.

[7] B. Wilson, 'An analysis of sect development', *American Sociological Review*, **24**, 1959, pp. 3–15.

[8] A. Rigby and B. S. Turner, 'Findhorn Community, centre of light: a sociological study of new forms of religion', *A Sociological Yearbook of Religion in Britain*, **5**, 1972, pp. 72–86.

[9] P. Worsley, *The Third World*, London, Weidenfeld & Nicolson, 1968, p. 268.

[10] M. Rodinson, *Israel, a colonial-settler state?*, New York, Monad Press, 1973.

[11] B. Bettelheim, *Children of the Dream*, New York, Macmillan, 1969; M. E. Spiro, *Kibbutz, venture in Utopia*, New York, Shocken, 1963; Y. Talman, *Family and Community in the Kibbutz*, Harvard, Harvard University Press, 1972.

[12] N. Davis, *Israel: Utopia Incorporated*, London, Zed Press, 1977.

[13] T. Shanin, 'The peasantry as a political factor', *The Sociological Review*, **14**(1), 1966, pp. 5–27.

[14] E. R. Wolf, *Sons of the Shaking Earth*, Chicago and London, University of Chicago Press, 1959; E. R. Wolf, *Peasant Wars of the Twentieth Century*, London, Faber & Faber, 1971.

[15] J. C. Scott, *The Moral Economy of the Peasant, rebellion and subsistence in South-east Asia*, New Haven and London, Yale University Press, 1976.

[16] B. Moore, *Social Origins of Dictatorship and Democracy, lord and peasant in the making of the modern world*, London, Allen Lane, 1967; S. R. Schram, *The Political Thought of Mao Tse-Tung*, New York, Paeger, 1969.

[17] L. Kolakowski, *Main Currents of Marxism, The Breakdown*, Vol. 3, Oxford, Clarendon Press, 1978, pp. 494ff.

[18] R. Israeli, *Muslims in China: a study in cultural confrontation*, London, Curzon Press, 1980.

[19] G. Dalton, *Economic Systems and Society, capitalism, communism and the Third World*, Harmondsworth, Penguin Books, 1974.

[20] S. Wong, *Sociology and Socialism in Contemporary China*, London, Routledge & Kegan Paul, 1979.

[21] J. L. Watson (ed.), *Class and Social Stratification in Post-revolutionary China*, Cambridge, Cambridge University Press, 1984.

[22] J. Peck, 'Why China "Turned West"', *The Socialist Register*, 1972, pp. 289–306; R. Medveder, 'The USSR and China: confrontation or detente', *New Left Review*, No. 142, 1983, pp. 5–29.

[23] F. Parkin, 'Class stratification in socialist societies', *British Journal of Sociology*, **20**(4), 1969, pp. 355–374.

[24] M. Matthews, *Privilege in the Soviet Union: a study of elite lifestyles under communism*, London, Allen & Unwin, 1978.

[25] O. Caroe, *Soviet Empire, the Turks of central Asia and Stalinism*, New York, St. Martin's Press, 1967; G. Chaliand (ed.), *People Without a Country*, London, Zed Press, 1980.

[26] D. Lane, *The End of Inequality? Stratification under State Socialism*, Harmondsworth, Penguin Books, 1971.

[27] J. Gardiner, 'Conflict, control and cleavage in the Chinese People's Republic' in R. Scase (ed.), *Industrial Society: class cleavage and control*, London, Allen & Unwin, 1977, pp. 191–202.

[28] J. Kolaja, *Workers' Councils, the Yugoslav experience*, London, Tavistock, 1965.

[29] K. Wittfogel, *Oriental Despotism, a comparative study of total power*, New Haven and London, Yale University Press, 1957.

[30] R. Bahro, *The Alternative in Eastern Europe*, London, NLB, 1978; M. Djilas, *The New Class, an analysis of the communist system*, London, Allen & Unwin, 1966; M. Djilas, *The Unperfect Society, beyond the new class*, London, Methuen, 1969; M. Schachtman, *The Bureaucratic Revolution*, London, Donald Press, 1962.

[31] J. Burnham, *The Managerial Revolution*, Harmondsworth, Penguin Books, 1945.

[32] R. Aron, *Progress and Disillusion, the dialectics of modern society*, Harmondsworth, Penguin Books, 1972.

[33] I. Szelenyi, 'Social inequalities in state socialist re-distributive economics', *International Journal of Comparative Sociology*, **19**(1–2), 1978, pp. 63–83.

[34] F. Feher, A. Heller and G. Markus, *Dictatorship Over Needs, an analysis of Soviet societies*, Oxford, Basil Blackwell, 1983, p. 45.

6

Towards Equality

EGALITARIANISM

It is often said that sociology is a value-free science of society which provides a descriptive account of the basic structures of human communities. Sociology does not make moral commentaries on the topics which are selected for study, but of course the reasons for choosing a particular area for analysis are guided by certain values. This distinction was basic to Weber's philosophy of social science in which he contrasted the notions of value neutrality and value relevance. While sociologists may have studied inequality in a value-neutral fashion, they have concentrated on inequality because of the relevance of this topic to moral debate and social policy. In this study we have seen that the British tradition of sociology in particular has taken the question of poverty and inequality as a fundamental feature of research from the surveys of B. S. Rowntree to the more recent research of R. M. Titmuss. Although social philosophers like R. H. Tawney were motivated by an overtly moral commitment to the problem of equality, it is interesting that modern sociologists have not taken the problem of explaining equality and our sense of fairness as significant issues. By concentrating on the nature of inequality, sociologists generally have failed to explain how equality and an egalitarian ideal might emerge in modern societies.

In this sociological inquiry, starting with the premise that all societies are unequal, I have identified certain historical changes which promote egalitarian ideas and institutions. The enhancement of equality is associated with an expanding concept of social participation which is brought about by the development of citizenship in Western societies from the eighteenth century. Citizenship as a doctrine starts in modern times with the quest of the bourgeois class for greater representation in society in opposition to aristocratic privilege. Legal citizenship has limited objectives, which are primarily to free the individual from arbitrary legal constraints. Legal citizenship was associated with an expansion of opportunity, namely to open the professions and public administration to entry by educational qualification. The movement for greater equality of condition was part of a wider political program by the urban working class through the institutions of bourgeois democracy to achieve some regulation of the capitalist economy. Social citizenship attempted to reform capitalism by legislation. The gradual development of universal provision for basic education, health and social security was a modest attempt to bring about an equality of condition. The expansion of the welfare state in the post-war period was an extension of social legislation which began in the 1870s. The cumulative effect of reformist legislation in terms of social security and social insurance is to change the nature of the cash nexus between capital and labour. Legislation on minimum wages, hours of work, employment of adults, work conditions, occupational safety and compensation for occupational accidents has never been entirely successful, especially in terms of implementation, but it has made the employee less vulnerable as a mere commodity on the labour market. Legislation for social citizenship to bring about a minimal equality of condition changed the nature of capitalism as a social system.

These changes do not fundamentally transform the economic basis of capitalism in terms of the private appropriation of wealth. While the family remained the social vehicle for the transfer of private property to male offspring, the patriarchal household continued to be a fundamental buttress of capitalist relations. The rich sent their children to public schools as a preparation for leadership in business, professions or government under the slogan of equality of opportunity. They resisted comprehensive schooling under the moral discourse of the parental right to control the education of their children. The wealthy protected private property, home ownership, private health and private insurance under the erstwhile revolutionary slogans of liberty and freedom. This is the paradox of capitalist society which, following Marshall's perspective, I have called a hyphenated system, because it combines a progressive expansion of egalitarian citizenship rights with the continuity of de facto inequalities in terms of class, status and power.

In his classic study, Tawney said that equality would begin to assume real significance once the principles of liberty, equality and fraternity began to operate on the factory floor. As we saw in the case of Sweden, a successful program of social reform (designed to change the conditions of social competition through equality of condition) can leave a society basically unequal in terms of power and wealth. A radical movement for social equality would attempt to guarantee equality of outcome by changing the economic basis of society either by abolishing private property or by ensuring that all essential services were free on demand. In this sense, citizenship would now embrace economic, in addition to legal and social, rights. The focus of these rights would be equal participation and control of the means of production. A socialist transformation of society would be a logical extension of the movement of citizenship as a process of expanding social participation. We can now express these relationships diagrammatically:

Equality	Citizenship	Level	Politics
opportunity	legal	person	liberalism
condition	social	society	reformism
outcome	economic	production	socialism

In this representation of the relationship between equality and citizenship, we can see that classical liberalism was a revolutionary movement to liberate the person from the fetters of legal restraint under feudalism. It gave rise to the notion of a career open to talent. Reformism attempted to change the conditions of competition in capitalism by the legislative management of social conditions. The provision of free school meals would be a clear, if mundane, illustration of reformism in terms of social citizenship. Finally, socialism attempts to bring about an equality of outcome by changing what is seen to be the real basis of inequality, namely the ownership and control of the productive basis of society. Socialism in these terms does not abandon the principles of legal and social citizenship; it has to presuppose and incorporate these more elementary systems of right.

Equality, especially equality of outcome, is very difficult to achieve and to sustain over any length of time for reasons which have been made clear by Durkheim, Weber and Dahrendorf. However, the question of difficulty should not be an irrefutable argument against a principle. No doubt bourgeois liberals were constantly warned that the achievement of careers open to talent would be terribly difficult to achieve. Social science evidence should properly lead us to feel deeply pessimistic about equality of outcome as an objective in the long run; however, there is an important difference between pessimism and fatalism.

PRECONDITIONS FOR EQUALITY

Although sociologists have largely ignored the problem of explaining the emergence of an egalitarian ideal, within political sociology there has been some discussion of the nature of democratic equality and the importance of an egalitarian society as the basis for an effective democratic political tradition. For example, in American political science, the development of egalitarianism was seen to be crucial to the stability of modern industrial capitalism [1]. Other writers have been concerned to explain the emergence of moral notions in children, especially notions concerning fairness and justice [2]. I have also argued in this study that there is an important debate about the origins of our sense of equality growing out of exchange theory. However, given the importance of equality to modern societies, it is remarkable that there is so little research on equality and little theoretical interest in the nature of equality and the explanation of its origins. In fact, A. de Tocqueville remains one of the few classical writers to have seriously investigated the modern roots of egalitarianism in the very structure of mass democracy [3]. Historical studies of the impact of market societies on personal liberties and social equality are clearly germane to our inquiry [4]. It remains the case, however, that direct studies of the idea of egalitarianism and conditions of equality are rare.

In the perspective of this study, I have associated the development of equality, both as a principle and as a practice, with violent upheavals of the social structure, which call into question particularistic and hierarchical relationships. In this respect, my approach depends heavily on Weber. The historical origins of equality are bound up with the preconditions for the development of rational capitalism — the occidental city, Roman law, a system of monetary exchange, administration by officials and a this-worldy religious ethnic. Equality requires equity in terms of the delivery of a service and the achievement of desirable standards of efficiency and reliability requires bureaucracy. Following Weber, it has also been argued that the expansion of citizenship was bound up with the struggle of social classes to achieve rights; these struggles were often more effective under conditions of war with external enemies.

Weber clearly associated the rise of modern citizenship with changes in the character of military relationships. Terms like '*plebs*'. '*popolo*' and '*burgerschaft*' are very different, but they 'designate the mass of citizens who do not pursue the knightly life' [5]. Democratization, that is egalitarian political rights, presupposes the social decline of an estate of privileged mean-at-arms. Furthermore,

> The basis of democratization is everywhere purely military in character; it lies in the rise of disciplined infantry, the *hoplites* of antiquity, the guild army in the middle ages . . . Military discipline meant the triumph of democracy because the community wished and was compelled to secure the cooperation of the non-

aristocratic masses and hence put arms, along with arms political power, into their hands. [6]

In the twentieth century, mass wars fought by conscripted civilians have provided the context within which the majority of the population was able to secure a limited equality of condition.

EGALITARIAN BELIEFS

The social-psychological conditions for the emergence of an egalitarian belief system have been debated in an important article ('On the structure of egalitarianism') by L. R. Della-Fave [7], who starts his argument with the interesting observation that, while America is an unequal society, even the poor do not support the idea that there should be greater equality in the distribution of income. Among black Americans in the lowest income category, only 27 per cent support egalitarianism in the distribution of wealth [8]. In order for a commitment to egalitarianism to emerge, certain important conditions must be present.

First, there has to be a strong sense of grievance of deprivation (whether this is absolute or relative). This sense of deprivation must be connected with a desire to change social circumstances in an objective way. Religious cults and millenarian movements can be regarded as symbolic transformations of reality in response to relative deprivation [9]. People must see feasible means for changing their actual circumstances. Second, deprived people must blame the system, not themselves. In America, the dominance of individualistic moral beliefs makes the emergence of egalitarianism problematic, since the emphasis on individual responsibility is prominent. In the context of individualism, the notion of equality of opportunity is quite consistent with this general belief, but a commitment to equality of outcome is unlikely. Thirdly, there has to be the belief that social justice requires equality. Fourth, egalitarianism is associated with a world-view which suggests that human nature can be changed and is not determined by biology or environment. By contrast, social groups who are in favour of retaining existing forms of inequality tend to regard human beings as evil and in need of permanent social control. Egalitarians have to argue against the view that inequality is inevitable because of some fixed human characteristic (such as selfishness). Finally, egalitarians have to overcome the notion that the cost of achieving equality is too great, because it would involve the destruction of other values, such as personal liberty. It is for this reason that the reformist option for gradualism is attractive because it breaks the connection between revolutionary violence and equality [10]; at least it is suggested that there is no necessary connection.

The point of the argument is to suggest that commitment to an egalitarian belief is cumulative; the logic of the process may be broken or disrupted at any stage. It also takes note of the fact that a commitment to equality of outcome as a belief will be highly deviant in a society where individualism is a relatively dominant belief. The existence of a socialist party to advocate such beliefs is likely to be important for the maintenance of a 'deviant' commitment to equality [11].

THE DRIFT TO EQUALITY

In this inquiry, I have suggested that equality emerges out of the active and conscious struggle of social groups to achieve social participation through citizenship rights. There are also certain processes in modern societies, especially at the level of culture, which undermine traditional distinctions between people by producing common sentiments and tastes. We could regard this levelling as an immanent force in popular culture.

In contemporary social theory an important contribution has been made to the analysis of cultural equality by E. Gellner in a neglected article on 'The social roots of egalitarianism' [12]. Within a wider framework, we can say that the egalitarian character of modern culture has been fundamental to Gellner's anthropological inquiries, especially with reference to the political importance of modern Islam [13]. Gellner argues that there are a number of important processes in modern industrial society which tend to bring about an egalitarian ideal, partly as a consequence of the decline of hierarchical social structures and a weakening of the cultures which traditionally legitimated inequality.

For example, modern industrial societies are characterized by a degree of social mobility which makes the enforcement of traditional forms of rank especially difficult. Occupational mobility is incompatible with a system of hereditary rank; but we may add to this claim the argument that geographical mobility also tends to liquidate conventional notions of hierarchical authority [14]. The movement of young people to the towns has been associated with the decline of parental authority and with the patriarchal dominance of the father within the traditional household. Socially mobile women in the nineteenth century discovered a new egalitarian ethic in the towns where, although they were economically exploited, they were able to avoid some aspects of patriarchal control [15]. Within the anonymous city, the control of the kin group no longer had social relevance and young people found themselves increasingly free from the ascriptive social regulations of the countryside.

Gellner also argues that the nature of contemporary work conditions and forms of technology create a bureaucratic hierarchy in the factory but nevertheless bring about a certain levelling of human experience and attitude. Modern work experience is typically characterized by fleeting, anonymous and shallow social relations which, combined with the experience of social mobility, undermine the more permanent hierarchies of pre-modern society. In addition, there is an important separation of home and work within industrial capitalism and the privacy of domestic space creates possibilities for the worker to experience a sense of egalitarian leisure outside the control and dominance of the employer or the state. While critical theorists have been hostile to the idea of bourgeois privacy, the separation of home and work actually creates a space for the development of personal autonomy and thereby contributes to the emergence of egalitarian culture. Of course, we could criticize Gellner's argument because it fails to take into acccount the sexual division of labour which occurs within the home; feminist theory would argue that women are extremely unequal in this domestic environment. Against these feminist arguments, it can be asserted that many features of modern capitalism, especially the involvement of women in work, have weakened patriarchal authority within the household. The whole structure of the modern household has been transformed and the decline of the nuclear family has contributed to the changing status of women in society; these changes plus the development of citizenship for women have brought about a more egalitarian culture within the household.

Gellner goes on to suggest that the development of the mass media and the emergence of modern consumerism have produced a leisure society where traditional standards of taste and the forms of cultural inequality associated with them have declined. The capacity of the working class to enjoy these new commodities has depended significantly on the growth of hire purchase, mortgages and other loan facilities. The development of this consumer society was associated with embourgeoisement; the British working class had the benefit of rising wages and full employment in the two decades following the Second World War which contributed to the evolution of a consumer culture. With the development of mass taste through advertising, established notions of elite culture have come under increasing attack. Conservative critics of modern culture have argued that there is an important role for an educated elite in modern society as the carrier of refined taste and cultivated opinion. In this view the levelling of culture brings about a deterioration of standards [16].

The growth of a mass consumer culture was closely related, historically and sociologically to the emergence of mass education and uniform training. This uniformity of training and socializing is an important ingredient of modern egalitarianism. While there has been an important growth in the division of labour with the increasing complexity of modern technology, there has also been the need for re-training and re-skilling. There is as a consequence no contradiction between the increasing diversity of socio-economic roles and the emergence of a relatively standardized educational experience, despite class differences. Within the university system, there is high prestige associated with unspecialized education, since this enhances the capacity for social and occupational mobility. Gellner's emphasis on the standardisation of knowledge and culture through the development of a national educational system would be a view which most educational sociologists would challenge. The conventional argument is that the institutional divisions within the British educational system reflect and reproduce the underlying difference between manual and non-manual occupational groups; that is, the school produces and reproduces the class distinctions which are deeply embedded within the wider community [17]. In support of Gellner's argument it can be claimed that there has been a far higher rate of social mobility than early critics of the English educational system had suggested [18]. While the London–Oxford–Cambridge axis still dominates British cultural life, the development of the new universities in provincial towns in the post-war period contributed to a regionalization of culture which in turn brought about a levelling of taste and culture in the middle classes. It can be argued that universities are inherently and necessarily conservative; they are the institutional bastions of existing inequalites in society. In fact, the university as an institution is organized around the problem of balancing the conservation of tradition and the production of innovation and novelty; universities stand in a contradictory relationship to the maintenance of a traditionally unequal culture [19]. However, the new universities, the Open University and the technical colleges did play a role in bringing higher education to a wider audience in post-war Britain.

I wish to extend and support Gellner's argument that there are underlying egalitarian trends in modern society by claiming that his argument should be seen as a positive analysis of mass society. Within the mainstream tradition of sociology, the concept of a mass society has generally been developed as a negative critique of modernity. The notion of a mass society has a long history and is often associated with right-wing criticism of industrial society [20]. Against this conservative critique, writers like E. Shils suggested that mass politics had a positive dimension, since the involvement of the majority of the population in the political process made elite political manipulation of power far more difficult and uncertain [21]. Following Shils's argument we can develop the notion of mass society to suggest, while modern societies are empirically unequal, they also contain distinctive processes which bring about a more egalitarian society through the growth of mass culture. In particular, mass society brings about a levelling of rank, culture and taste which undermines many traditional forms of status, attitude and lifestyle.

Consumer culture can have a certain liberating quality. For example, while it is common to bemoan the decline of the neighbourhood shop, the growth of the department store and the supermarket has extended the range of choices open to working-class people, but more importantly has made the delivery of commodities effective and efficient. These institutions have reduced the amount of time which individuals are forced to commit to the task of purchasing goods and services. More significantly they have transformed our preception of the world and brought about a more egalitarian culture, grounded in modern consumption [22]. Romantic attitudes towards the local shop should not blind us to the repressive atmosphere of these petty bourgeois institutions which traditionally held a monopoly over local consumption. The impersonality of the superstore brings with it a certain equalization and levelling of modern consumption. The customers may be faceless, but at least they are all equally faceless.

In more general terms, the existence of mass culture and mass consumption has challenged the traditional logic of elite culture among the aristocracy and the high bourgeoisie. Artistic reproduction (along with the camera and the cinema) has transformed our experience of the world, but mass reproduction has also rendered impossible a traditional art culture based upon the authentic work of art by the master of an artistic tradition [23]. The architecture of modern cities, and especially the building design of modern suburbia, has also brought about a standardization of culture which has implicit within it an egalitarian distribution of space. Although the middle-class architecture of the bungalow has been the object of considerable criticism from art historians and urban sociologists, suburbia and suburban culture not only represented an important development of democratic equality, but also made possible an enhancement of personal privacy which, as Gellner had indicated, is an important element of individual freedom and equality [24].

Modern egalitarianism owes a great deal to contemporary means of mass transportation. The development of the railways in the nineteenth century made cheap transport available to the masses and helped to remove immobility, provincialism and isolation of the traditional subordinate working class. The railway made possible the weekend excursion and the working-class holiday. The railway system in Britain therefore eventually gave rise to the popular culture of the seaside which was in itself a levelling and egalitarian culture. The railway excursion opened up a new world of experience and leisure for families on low incomes. For example, in 1848 during Whit Week one hundred and sixteen thousand passangers left Manchester on cheap excursions and throughout the late Victorian period, excursion trains provided a unique opportunity for excitement, fun and adventure in working-class holiday sites such as Scarborough and Blackpool [25]. In the twentieth century the egalitarian implications of mass transport were further developed with the arrival of individualized transport in the form of the Ford motor car. Ownerhsip of the motor car became, along with the ownerhsip of a home, an essential feature of modern democracies. Although in contemporary social theory the motor car has become the object of extensive criticism because it is destructive of the natural and social environment, this criticism has masked the political importance of the motor car as a symbol and instrument of personal autonomy. By concentrating on Fordism as a method of managerial control over the worker, critics have neglected the liberating quality of personalized transport.

These developments in transport, communication and consumption provided the institutional framework for the growth of the mass media in the post-war period. Radio and television contributed to the evolution of a uniform culture for all social classes. Modern systems of communication can of course be seen as merely an elaboration of certain social changes from the nineteenth century with the growth of a mass reading public and the development of a national system of newspapers [26]. The arrival of radio and television as means of mass communication represented in fact a distinct departure from traditional forms of communication through the written word. It has been argued that television brought about a passive reception of information which was distinctively privatized; some critics therefore deny that television represents communication, since it involves a one-way transmission of information. The development of a television culture was part of an entirely new social structure which was simultaneously mobile and also home-centred [27].

Modern media have been criticized on the grounds that they have trivialized culture, undermined traditional standards of excellence and encouraged a consumer culture based upon hedonism, sex and violence. Left-wing and right-wing criticism often converges on the idea that the media are essentially dangerous because they either destroy traditional values or because they subordinate the working class to a dominant ideology. These criticisms of the television often fail to take into account the extensive findings of sociological research which suggest that the television and the media generally have not had significantly negative effects on individuals; the media are received through the network of existing attitudes and opinions which are resistant to media manipulation

[28]. Sociologists have too frequently concentrated on the negative effects of modern systems of communication and they have neglected the important role of television in modern democracies in disseminating information and opinion. The public broadcasting system has also catered to minority and specialized interests; criticism of the media often fails to differentiate between commercial and public channels. In the British context, the BBC has played a major educational role in establishing standards of taste in the arts and in providing an arena for public debate and evaluation of politics and social policy.

Industrial society produces, especially at the level of culture, an egalitarian ideal which develops out of the set of institutions which we collectively call 'mass society'. Furthermore, popular and mass culture have a positive role to play in a democracy because it is in mass culture that many of the traditional hierarchies of status and custom have been eroded or eradicated. This is not to suggest that Britain or any other industrial society is egalitarian. Indeed I have shown, in terms of a variety of social dimensions, that industrial societies are fundamentally unequal. However, sociologists have too frequently concentrated exclusively on inequality to the neglect of equality. We should be sensitive to those processes in culture and structure which bring about either a sense of justice or an actual situation of interpersonal equality.

Through this sociological inquiry I have suggested that inequality and equality are the woof and warp of all social life. Dahrendorf noted that since all societies have norms, inequality in terms of the evaluation of difference will be permanent and pervasive. The same issues arise in the case of common culture. Human beings are not simply passive recipients of culture; rather they are involved in countless acts of evaluation, classification and assessment. In short, everyday life involves the exercise of discriminating taste, which in turn brings about hierarchies of artifacts and persons. Taste is part of a hierarchy of cultural inequalities:

> Taste is an acquired disposition to 'differentiate' and 'appreciate', as Kant says — in other words, to establish and mark differences by a process of distinction which is not (or not necessarily) a distinct knowledge . . . Taste is a practical mastery of distribution which makes it possible to sense or intuit what is likely (or unlikely) to befall — and therefore to benefit — an individual occupying a given position in social space. [29]

The exercise of taste creates distinctions which separate persons in terms of hierarchies of cultural prestige. Every practical task of the mundane world — brushing our hair, wearing a shirt, eating our lunch, holding a cup — is subject to and expressive of discriminations of taste by which we can be ranked. Since distinctions of taste are endemic, there could never be a completely uniform, egalitarian and general culture. The egalitarian implication of mass culture will always have the limit of taste.

CONCLUSION

All human societies are unequal in terms of class, status and power. However, social stratification exists in socialist societies as much as in capitalism. The removal of economic inequality in state-socialist societies may well create the circumstances for an intensification of inequality in status and prestige. Positive attempts to eradicate inequality are often undermined by the paradoxical relationship between personal liberty and social equality. It is important, however, to distinguish between equality of opportunity and other forms of equality. While most democracies have successfully achieved some level of equality of opportunity and of condition, it would appear sociologically problematic to establish a society in which equality of outcome could be achieved without the imposition of authoritarian rule. Even equality of condition requires significant inroads into the organization of the family, especially with respect to the inheritance of wealth. However, the classic contradiction between individualism and equality is often misplaced, since the achievement of personal development in the form of individuality may well require significant contributions from the state and the community. Throughout this inquiry I have attempted to link together the importance of citizenship in the modern polity with the problem of equality in relation to economic structures. In contemporary society there often appears to be a contradiction between the quest for equality at the level of politics and the continuity of the social division of labour and private property. Whereas the economy generates inequalites between individuals who compete for scarce resources, the political system works on the basis of democratic equality in terms of individual rights. This contradiction between politics and economics tends to destabilize modern governments.

Although many of these conclusions might be regarded as pessimistic, I have identified a number of processes promoting equality in human societies. First, the sense of justice or equity appears to be a necessary feature of social relations insofar as society is constituted by reciprocity and exchange. There is therefore a fundamental principle of fair exchange which emerges from the structure of society. Secondly, I have argued that personal consumption in capitalism is the economic side of democratic citizenship. Politics is not simply coercive control but also a set of institutions which enable people to achieve desired goals. Similarly consumption is not simply the binding of the individual to what Marx regarded as the necessity of nature, since consumption has a variety of quite positive and liberating functions. Various aspects of mass consumption bring about an egalitarian ethos and undermine traditional aspects of structural inequality, especially inequality of status. Thirdly, social groups and social movements successfully mobilize to achieve substantive social rights to expand participation through citizenship.

The forms of equality which we enjoy in modern democracy are to some extent the consequences of violent or radical action on the part of subordinate groups to achieve a more equitable distribution of wealth and power. The working-class movement, through political parties and trade unionism, contributed significantly to the development of welfare rights, particularly under war-time conditions. In more recent times, the women's movement has also brought about a significant transformation of the legal status of women and children in the community. The movement for racial equality would be another example. However, some causes of modern egalitarianism may be less obvious and intentional. Some features of equality may be the consequence of the spread of popular culture through the mass media. Common culture is often seen to be crude and popular taste is often criticized for its vulgarity. However, we should remind ourselves that the word 'vulgar' comes from the latin *vulgus* which meant the 'common people'. Perhaps equality requires a certain vulgarity in opposition to elitist principles of hierarchical prestige, privilege and power.

REFERENCES

[1] D. Bell, *The End of Ideology*, New York, Free Press, 1960; D. Apter, *The Politics of Modernization*, Chicago and London, University of Chicago Press, 1965; S. M. Lipset, *Political Man*, London, Mercury Books, 1963.

[2] J. Piaget, *The Moral Judgement of the Child*, London, Routledge & Kegan Paul, 1968; K. Menzies, *Talcott Parsons and the Social Image of Man*, London, Routledge & Kegan Paul, 1976, Ch. 6.

[3] A. de Tocqueville, *Democracy in America*, London, Oxford University Press, 1946; I. Zeitlin, *Liberty, Equality and Revolution in Alexis de Tocqueville*, Boston, Little, Brown & Co., 1971.

[4] K. Polanyi, *The Great Transformation*, Boston, Beacon Press, 1957.

[5] M. Weber, *General Economic History*, New Brunswick, Transaction Books, 1981, p. 324.

[6] Ibid., pp. 324–325.

[7] L. R. Della-Fave, 'On the structure of egalitarianism', *Social Problems*, **22**, 1974, pp. 199–213.

[8] J. Feagin, 'God helps those who help themselves', *Psychology Today*, **6**, 1972, pp. 101–129.

[9] V. Lantenari, *The Religions of the Oppressed, a study of modern messianic cults*, London, MacGibbon & Kee, 1963.

[10] L. T. Hobhouse, *Liberalism*, New York, H. Holt & Co., 1911.

[11] F. Parkin. *Class Inequality and Political Order*, London, MacGibbon & Kee, 1971.

[12] E. Gellner, 'The social roots of egalitarianism', *Dialectics and Humanism*, **4**, 1979, pp. 27–43.

[13] E. Gellner, *Thought and Change*, London Weidenfeld & Nicolson, 1964; E. Gellner, *Muslim Society*, Cambridge, Cambridge University Press, 1981.

[14] D. Lerner, *The Passing of Traditional Society, modernizing the Middle East*, New York, The Free Press, 1958.

[15] E. Shorter, *The Making of the Modern Family*, London, Fontana, 1977.

[16] T. S. Eliot, *Notes Towards the Definition of Culture*, London, Faber & Faber, 1948.

[17] B. Jackson, *Streaming, an education system in miniature*, London, Routledge & Kegan Paul, 1964, and O. Banks, *Parity and Prestige in English Secondary Education*, London, Routledge & Kegan Paul, 1955.

[18] A. H. Halsey, *Change in British Society*, Oxford, Oxford University Press, 1978, Ch. 6.

[19] E. Shils, *Tradition*, London, Faber & Faber, 1981, pp. 179ff.

[20] S. Giner, *Mass Society*, London, Martin Robertson, 1976.

[21] E. Shils, 'The Theory of Mass Society', *Diogenes*, **39**, 1962, pp. 45–66.

[22] J. W. Ferry, *A History of the Department Store*, New York, Macmillan, 1960.

[23] W. Benjamin, 'The work of art in the age of mechanical reproduction' in *Illuminations*, London, Fontana, 1973, pp. 219–254.

[24] J. M. Richards, *The Castles on the Ground, the autonomy of suburbia*, London, John Murray, 1973; A. D. King, *The Bungalow, the production of a global culture*, London, Routledge & Kegan Paul, 1984.

[25] J. Walvin, *Leisure and Society 1830–1950*, London, Longman, 1978.

[26] R. Williams, *The Long Revolution*, London, Chatto & Windus, 1961.

[27] R. Williams, *Television, technology and cultural form*, London, Fontana, 1974, p. 26.

[28] D. McQuail (ed.), *Sociology of Mass Communications*, Harmondsworth, Penguin Books, 1972.

[29] P. Bourdieu, *Distinction, a social critique of the judgement of taste*, London, Routledge & Kegan Paul, 1984, p. 466.

Bibliographical Essay

There are a number of general guides and introductions to the literature on social stratification; these provide a broad overview of the sociological literature on the principal dimensions of inequality, namely class, status and power. These include A. Béteille (ed.), *Social Inequality, Selected Readings*, Harmondsworth, Penguin Books, 1969; B. Barber, *Social Stratification, a comparative analysis of structure and process*, New York and Burlingane, Harcourt, Brace & World, 1957; R. Bendix and S. M. Lipset (eds.), *Class Status and Power, a reader in social stratification*, New York, Free Press of Glencoe, 1953; R. K. Kelsall and H. M. Kelsall, *Stratification, an essay on class and inequality*, London and New York, Longman, 1974; A. Giddens and D. Held (eds.), *Classes, Power and Conflict, Classical and Contemporary Debates*, London, Macmillan Press, 1982; F. Parkin (ed.), *A Social Analysis of Class Structure*, London, Tavistock, 1974; and finally for a collection of essays dealing with the functionalist theory of stratification there is M. M. Tumin (ed.), *Readings on Social Stratification*, Englewood Cliffs, New Jersey, Prentice-Hall, 1970.

A number of classical texts deal with the general theme of power, privilege and inequality. The most useful would include T. H. Marshall, *Class Citizenship and Social Development*, Chicago and London, University of Chicago Press, 1977; G. E. Lenski, *Power and Privilege, a theory of social stratification*, New York, McGraw-Hill, 1966; R. Dahrendorf, *Essays in the Theory of Society*, London, Routledge & Kegan Paul, 1968; A. Giddens, *The Class Structure of the Advanced Societies*, London, Hutchinson, 1973.

There are in addition a variety of publications which deal more specifically with the topic of equality and inequality. While there are a great variety of such texts, the most useful in a sociological framework would be H. J. Gans, *More Equality*, New York, Vintage Books, 1974; A. Béteille, *The Idea of Natural Inequality and Other Essays*, Delhi, Oxford University

Press, 1983; W. Letwin (ed.), *Against Equality, readings on economic and social policy*, London and Basingstoke, Macmillan Press, 1983.

Some of the philosophical aspects of equality and inequality are considered by R. W. Wollheim and I. Berlin in *The Proceeding of the Aristotelian Society*, New Series, vol. 61, 1956, pp. 281–326.

The problem of equality is closely related to questions of equity and justice. The classic discussion of this issue in recent times is by J. Rawls, *A Theory of Justice*, Oxford, Oxford University Press, 1972. For a discussion of Rawls it is useful to consult A. Flew, *The Politics of Procrustes, contradictions of enforced equality*, New York , Prometheus Books, 1981. There is also the influential study by M. Ginsberg, *On Justice in Society*, Harmondsworth, Penguin Books, 1965. Finally there is the work of R. H. Tawney, *Equality*, New York, Barnes & Noble, 1931.

Inequality of power is clearly fundamental to social stratification. In political sociology, the unequal distribution of power is often considered in terms of the role of political elites in modern societies. The classical work on elites is derived from G. Mosca (1858–1941) and V. Pareto (1848–1923). A valuable commentary on their contribution is provided in J. H. Meisel (ed.), *Pareto and Mosca*, Englewood Cliffs, New Jersey, Prentice-Hall, 1965. An influential study of America is C. Wright Mills, *The Power Elite*, New York, Oxford University Press, 1959. On elites in other societies, the student should consult J. Higley, D. Deacon and D. Smart, *Elites in Australia*, London, Routledge & Kegan Paul, 1979; J. Higley, G. L. Field and K. Groholt, *Elite Structure and Ideology, a theory with applications to Norway*, New York, Columbia University Press, 1976; and P. Stanworth and A. Giddens, *Elites and the British Class Structure*, Cambridge, Cambridge University Press, 1974. A general discussion of elite theory can be found in T. Bottomore, *Elites and Society*, London, Watts, 1964.

We can consider equality along a number of dimensions (wealth, power, privilege, ethnicity, gender and age). A variety of texts deal with specific features of equality and the student should consult the following: A. B. Atkinson, *Unequal Shares, wealth in Britain*, Harmondsworth, Penguin Books, 1972; A. B. Atkinson, *The Economics of Inequality*, Oxford, Clarendon Press, 1975; J. L. Roach and J. K. Roach (eds.), *Poverty, Selected Readings*, Harmondsworth, Penguin Books, 1972; W. D. Rubinstein (ed.), *Wealth and the Wealthy in the modern world*, London, Croom Helm, 1980; R. Dahrendorf, *Class and Class Conflict in an Industrial Society*, London, Routledge & Kegan Paul, 1959; D. H. Wrong, *Skeptical Sociology*, London, Heinemann, 1977, Chapter 10; T. J. Johnson, *Professions and Power*, London and Basingstoke, Macmillan Press, 1972; A. Schlegal (ed.), *Sexual Stratification*, New York, Columbia University Press, 1977; P. R. Sanday, *Female Power and Male Dominance, on the origins of sexual inequality*, Cambridge, Cambridge University Press, 1981; R. L. Blumberg, 'A general theory of gender stratification' in R. Collins (ed.), *Sociological Theory 1984*, San Francisco, Jossey-Bass, 1984, pp. 23–101; J. Rex, *Race Relations in Sociological Theory*, London, Weidenfeld & Nicolson, 1970; L. Dumont, *Homo Hierarchicus, an essay on the caste system*, Chicago, Chicago University Press, 1970; S. de Beauvoir, *Old Age*, Harmondsworth, Penguin Books, 1977.

On various dimensions of inequality, the supply of housing is a crucial element of social stratification. As a general introduction to urban sociology, the reader may consider R. Sennett (ed.), *Classic Essays on the Culture of Cities*, Englewood Cliffs, New Jersey, Prentice-Hall, 1969, P. Saunders, *Social Theory and the Urban Question*, London, Hutchinson, 1981 and M. Castells, *City, Class and Power*, London, Macmillan, 1978. On the specific issue of housing inequality, J. Rex, 'The concept of housing class and the sociology of race relations', *Race*, vol. 12, 1971, pp. 218–223, and J. Rex and R. Moore, *Race, Community and Conflict*, London, Oxford University Press, 1967.

Of the various dimensions of inequality, the sociological analysis of social class is probably the most developed, both theoretically and empirically. There are some useful introductory commentaries on class and class relations in modern society and these would include: T. B. Bottomore, *Classes in Modern Society*, London, Allen & Unwin, 1965; T. B. Bottomore, *Elites and Society*, Harmondsworth, Penguin Books, 1966; G. D. H. Cole, *Studies in Class Structure*, London, Routledge & Kegan Paul, 1955; S. Ossowski, *Class Structure in the Social Consciousness*, London, Routledge & Kegan Paul, 1963.

In more recent times the complexity of the Marxist and Weberian analysis of social class is reflected in N. Abercrombie and J. Urry, *Capital, Labour and the Middle Classes*, London, Allen & Unwin, 1983; A. Giddens and G. Mackenzie (eds.), *Social Class and the Division of Labour, essays in honour of Ilya Neustadt*, Cambridge, Cambridge University Press, 1982; A. Cottrell, *Social Classes in Marxist Theory*, London, Routledge & Kegan Paul, 1984; N. Poulantzas, *Political Power and Social Classes*, London, N. L. B. and Sheed & Ward, 1973; F. Parkin, *Marxism and Class Theory, a bourgeois critique*, London, Tavistock, 1979.

We can also consider inequality comparatively and the following represent a collection of important studies of social stratification in a variety of societies. In the case of Britain, there are the following range of texts: J. Urry, and J. Wakeford (eds.), *Power in Britain, sociological readings*, London, Heinemann, 1973; W. G. Runciman, *Relative Deprivation and Social Justice, a study of attitudes to social inequality in 20th century England*, London, Routledge & Kegan Paul, 1966; B. Jackson and D.

Marsden, *Education and the Working Class*, Harmondsworth, Penguin Books, 1966; J. Westergaard and H. Resler, *Class In Capitalist Society, a study of contemporary Britain*, London, Heinemann, 1975.

There are also a number of valuable studies of inequality in Australia. The student may wish to consult A. Daniel, *Power, Privilege and Prestige: occupations in Australia*, Sydney, Longman Cheshire, 1983; R. W. Connell and T. H. Irving, *Class Structure in Australian History, documents, narrative and argument*, Melbourne, Longman Cheshire, 1980; J. S. Western, *Social Inequality in Australian Society*, Melbourne, Macmillan,1983; J. Martin, *The Ethnic Dimension*, Sydney, Allen & Unwin, 1981; S. Encel, *Equality and Authority*, Melbourne, Cheshire, 1970.

On contemporary Europe in general, there is M. S. Archer and S. Giner (eds.), *Contemporary Europe, Class Status and Power*, London, Weidenfeld & Nicolson, 1971. On the working class in France and Britain, there are two influential studies by D. Gallie, *In Search of the New Working Class, automation and social integration within the capitalist enterprise*,Cambridge, Cambridge University Press, 1978 and *Social Inequality and Class radicalism in France and Britain*, Cambridge, Cambridge University Press, 1983.

Various aspects of inequality in North America are considered by J. H. Turner and C. Starnes, *Inequality, Privilege and Poverty in America*, Santa Monica, California, Goodyear, 1976. For a general overview, the student should consider M. Harrington, *The Other America*, New York, Macmillan, 1962; J. Huber and W. Form, *Income and Ideology*, New York, Free Press, 1973; S. M. Lipset, *The First New Nation*, Garden City, Doubleday, 1967; M. Milner, *The Illusion of Equality*, San Francisco, Jossey-Bass, 1972. The classic study of status groups was published in W. L. Warner and P. S. Lunt, *The Social Life of a Modern Community*, New Haven, Yale University Press, 1947. There is also C. W. Mills, *White Collar, the American middle classes*, New York, Oxford University Press, 1951, and W. F. Whyte, *The Organization Man*, New York, Simon & Schuster, 1956. Finally, an influential approach to a subculture is presented in W. F. Whyte, *Street Corner Society, the social structure of an Italian slum*, Chicago, Chicago University Press, 1961.

Racial inequality in America with special reference to black Americans has been analysed in T. Parsons and K. B. Clark (eds.), *The Negro American*, Boston, Beacon Press, 1965, and the whole problem of ethnic stratification is analysed in N. Glazer, *Ethnic Dilemmas 1964–1982*, Cambridge, Mass., Harvard University Press, 1983. The history of legislation with respect to civil rights is discussed in M. Berger, *Equality by Statute, the revolution in civil rights*, Garden City, New York, Anchor Books, 1978. The social system of stratification in Canadian society received its classic statement in J. Porter, *The Vertical Mosaic*, Toronto, University of Toronto Press, 1965. Finally, various features of ethnic and class inequality in Islamic societies of the Middle East are discussed in B. S. Turner, *Capitalism and Class in the Middle East*, London, Heinemann, 1984.

There is also the complex and protracted question of social stratification in state-socialist societies. The following studies would provide the student of inequality with a useful guide to the main parameters of this debate: D. Lane, *The End of Inequality? stratification under state socialism*, Harmondsworth, Penguin Books, 1971; D. Lane, *Soviet Economy and Society*, Oxford, Blackwell, 1985; W. Wesolowski, *Classes, Strata and Power*, London, Routledge & Kegan Paul, 1979; W. D. Connor, *Socialism, Politics and Equality, hierarchy and change in eastern Europe and the U.S.S.R.*, New York, Columbia University Press, 1979.

The problem of inequality in society leads into a discussion of the legitimation of stratification and hence to an analysis of the role of ideology in societies. For a general discussion of the nature of ideology there are a number of valuable introductory texts such as: N. Abercrombie, S. Hill and B. S. Turner, *The Dominant Ideology Thesis*, London, Allen & Unwin, 1980, and J. Larrain, *Marxism and Ideology*, London, Macmillan, 1983. The following studies deal more specifically with working-class attitudes towards equality, fairness and the distribution of rewards: C. Chamberlain, *Class Consciousness in Australia*, Sydney, Allen & Unwin, 1983; M. Mann, *Consciousness and Action amongst the Western Working Class*, London Macmillan, 1973; H. Newby, *The Deferential Worker*, Harmondsworth, Penguin, 1979; R. Sennett and J. Cobb, *The Hidden Injuries of Class*, Cambridge, Cambridge University Press, 1972 and R. Hoggart, *The Uses of Literacy* London, Chatto & Windus, 1957.

It is often argued that modern forms of radical egalitarianism conflict with the liberal philosophical tradition, especially since it is argued there is an inherent contradiction between individual rights and social equality. A number of recent studies have addressed the question of individualism from a sociological point of view and these include S. Lukes, *Individualism*, Oxford, Blackwell, 1979; A. Macfarlane, *The Origins of English Individualism*, Oxford, Blackwell, 1978; C. B. Macpherson, *The Political Theory of Possessive Individualism, Hobbes to Locke*, Oxford, Clarendon Press, 1962. The relationship between individualism and Protestant religion is discussed in B. S. Turner, *Religion and Social Theory, a materialist perspective*, London, Heinemann, 1983, Chapter 7.

An important dimension of equality is equality before the law and this feature of impartiality and fairness has been discussed in the sociology of law and in a number of recent contributions to legal history. Some historical features of equality under the common law tradition are discussed in D.

Hay, P. Linebaugh, J. Rule and E. P. Thompson, *Albion's Fatal Tree, crime and society in 18th century England*, Harmondsworth, Penguin Books, 1977, and A. Macfarlane, *The Justice and the Mare's Ale, law and disorder in 17th century England*, Oxford, Blackwell, 1981. The question of socialism and legality are discussed in P. Carlen an M. Collinson (eds.), *Radical Issues in Criminology*, Oxford, Martin Robertson, 1980, and T. Campbell, *The Left and Rights*, London, Routledge & Kegan Paul, 1983. The nature of civil rights in modern Britain has been considered from a variety of perspectives in P. Wallington (ed.), *Civil Liberties 1984*, Oxford, Martin Robertson, 1984. Civil rights are an important feature of the nature of the democratic process and aspects of citizenship, democracy and equality are considered in D. F. Thompson, *The Democratic Citizen, Social Science and Democratic Theory in the 20th Century*, Cambridge, Cambridge University Press, 1970.

Finally, questions of equality, equity and fairness emerge significantly in criminology, penology, economic theory, exchange relations and the sociology of tansactions and social exchange. In this particular context, the reader may wish to consider a number of significant contributions to the theory of social exchange in P. M. Blau, *Exchange and Power in Social Life*, New York, John Wiley, 1964; G. C. Homans, *Social Behaviour, its elementary forms*, New York, Harcourt, Brace & World, 1961; P. Ekeh, *Social Exchange Theory, the two traditions*, London, Heinemann, 1974; N. J. Smelser, *The Sociology of Economic Life*, Englewood Cliffs, New Jersey, Prentice-Hall, 1976. Many of the theoretical issues behind exchange theory, functionalism and social stratification are analysed in T. Bottomore and R. Nisbet (eds.), *A History of Sociological Analysis*, London, Heinemann, 1979.

Finally, in recent years a number of dictionaries of sociology have appeared which contain extensive entries in questions relating to class, power, status, rights and equality. These include: N. Abercrombie, S. Hill and B. S. Turner, *The Penguin Dictionary of Sociology*, London, Allen Lane, 1984; T. Bottomore (ed.), *A Dictionary of Marxist Thought*, Oxford, Blackwell, 1983; M. Mann (ed.), *The Macmillan Student Encylopaedia of Sociology*, London, Macmillan, 1983, R. Scruton, *A Dictionary of Political Thought*, London, Macmillan, 1982, and A. Kuper and J. Kuper (eds.), *The Social Science Encyclopedia*, London, Routledge & Kegan Paul, 1985.

Index

31
36
115.